Fantasy Football for Smart People

How to Win at Daily Fantasy Sports

Jonathan Bales
Founder of RotoAcademy
Co-Founder of Fantasy Labs
DraftKings Pro

Table of Contents
Fantasy Football for Smart People
How to Win at Daily Fantasy Sports

I. The Introductory Chapter to My Book

There's not much that's useful in this chapter. I feel bad even calling it a 'chapter,' to be honest. If this were a meal, this section wouldn't even be an appetizer. It would be like maybe some bread that's been sitting in the back that they bring out to everyone. But not really good bread with olive oil and stuff—just like hard, stale bread that you take one bite out of and then set down and then maybe give another chance later in the meal to soak up the sauce from your linguine because you think maybe you were too harsh on the bread earlier, but you realize it's even worse than you thought because you were really hungry when you sat down and it *still* tasted really shitty. I guess I'm saying I'd probably just skip it if I were you.

II. My Approach to Daily Fantasy ~~Football~~ Sports

This is the appetizer, and the appetizer can sometimes be the best part of a meal. In this chapter, I discuss broad daily fantasy strategy that becomes the foundation from which you can apply data found later in the book. This includes:

Employing a contrarian approach to DFS
Using game theory in daily fantasy sports
Exploiting public psychology
Developing an "antifragile" game plan
Probability and visualizing ranges of outcomes
Harnessing correlational effects in the NFL

III. Into the Lab: Testing Daily Fantasy Football Strategies

Working with our tools at Fantasy Labs, I examine historical pricing and performance data to determine how to best construct daily fantasy football lineups. You'll learn:

Whether or not streaky play exists and can predict success
How much Vegas lines matter for each position
How player/position consistency should alter your strategy
When to be price-sensitive
How to account for the impact of division games

IV. A Numbers Game: The Data on What's Really Winning Leagues

Utilizing data from DraftKings, I examine which strategies are the most profitable in daily fantasy football, including:

Which positions to use in the flex based on the league
How the most successful players allocate their cap space
How ownership affects GPP success
If you should stack teammates in cash games
The average scores needed to cash in each league type

V. The Ultimate List of Daily Fantasy Heuristics

A very long list of general daily fantasy heuristics, generated using research and data from the book

VI. Sample from "Daily Fantasy Pros Reveal Their Money-Making Secrets"

An excerpt on advanced tournament play with Al_Smizzle

Postface

I. The Intro Chapter to My Book

"Any time scientists disagree, it's because we have insufficient data. Then we can agree on what kind of data to get; we get the data; and the data solves the problem. Either I'm right, or you're right, or we're both wrong. And we move on. That kind of conflict resolution does not exist in politics or religion."

Neil deGrasse Tyson

I'm about to share something with you that no one outside of my home season-long fantasy football league has ever seen. It's sort of sick and extremely embarrassing.

First, a little background. I've run a fantasy football league since I was a sophomore in high school. It's a bunch of friends and family, including my dad, uncles, and brothers. Actually, I'm nine years older than my youngest brother (Justin), meaning he was seven-years old when the league was formed. He and another brother (Jason)—just a year older— had a team together.

Quick side story: This league was started back in the day when there really wasn't much going on with fantasy football. I think there was probably some league software available online, but we did everything by hand: all scoring, waiver wire moves...everything. When someone wanted to pick up a new player, they had to email the group and then I would approve it.

So one day my cousin emailed in that he was dropping Terrell Owens for Diet Pepsi Machine. If you don't know what Diet Pepsi Machine is then I don't know what to tell you; maybe get out once in a while. Or actually stay in more, idk.

So he emails in that he's dropping the top wide receiver in the league for a soda machine, and literally 60 seconds later we get an email from Jason and Justin:

"We want to drop Troy Hambrick for T.O."

I didn't have the heart to tell a seven and eight-year old that someone in our league didn't literally drop Terrell Owens for a fucking Pepsi machine. I did have the heart to trade them Laveranues Coles and Keenan McCardell for Marvin Harrison, although I think age seven is about the time you start making +EV decisions for yourself. Plus, together they were 15. But that's for another time.

Anyway, back to the original story. The embarrassing one. A few years later, I took down the total-points championship for my league. Again. And I lost in a head-to-head playoff match. Again. This is the email I sent out the night I lost.

> *Dear Fantasy Owners,*
>
> *I regret to inform you that I will be stepping down as Commissioner and as an owner in the fantasy football league at the conclusion of this season. There are a multitude of factors that are at play here, all of which are related to my declining sense of enjoyment and pride from playing the game. While I will always have a place in my heart for fantasy football, I loathe how it has affected the actual game of football. I, like most of you, find myself rooting for "meaningless" touchdowns and yards that have absolutely no effect on the outcome of a football game. Fantasy football is exciting, but focusing on the nuances of an intense matchup without worrying about why my wide receiver is on the sideline, for example, is far more exhilarating.*

Another reason I am retiring from fantasy football, and perhaps the strongest, is the inherent luck involved in the game. Despite doing everything necessary to win, I will not be in the championship of the playoffs this season. I have been the total-points leader all six years the league has been in existence, yet I have won a playoff championship just once. Something is wrong there. While luck is a component of all parts of life, its involvement in fantasy football has become far too great for me to handle.

Tonight, I finished third of four teams in the first round of the playoffs. I have no problem losing to TJ's team, which is stacked and got hot at the right time. He suffered injuries and other setbacks early in the season, but he built his squad the right way. Losing to Jason's team, however, is a tragedy. When my team, loaded with talent from top to bottom, finishes behind a team forced to start Brandon Jackson, Randy McMichael, and Mike Thomas, something is seriously, seriously wrong. Are Jackson, McMichael, and Thomas championship-caliber names to you? In those same spots, I started LeSean McCoy, Vernon Davis, and Steven Jackson. Truly sickening.

Some may point out that I started Johnny Knox as my No. 3 receiver—a player who clearly underperformed this season. That move, which nearly got me into the championship, was a calculated one on my part. It came just before the 4pm games yesterday, when I knew I was behind. I sat Brandon Lloyd in favor of Knox, as I knew the upside which the Cutler-Knox duo provided me was necessary to obtain the win. Those little moves are a major reason I've been so successful in fantasy football. They add up, and it's both disheartening and nauseating that an owner who starts Jackson, McMichael, and Thomas in the playoffs is able to out-point an owner shrewd enough to make those types of moves.

I am confident that many of you will label me a poor loser, selfish, or just an asshole. All of those things are spot on. But I'm a bitter, selfish asshole who wins fantasy football, and one who should be in the championship this season. I've realized the luck involved in fantasy football is far too great to justify the time and energy I invest into it.

I will hand over Commissioner duties to a deserving owner at the end of the season, and if anyone knows of someone who would like to take over my team, let me know. Just make sure they're willing to take over a powerhouse—a team that is truly the perfect balance of young, rising prospects and proven veterans—and see it lose to a team starting a backup running back, a backup tight end, and the No. 3 receiving option on a run-heavy team.

Jon

So what was the point of publishing that email? Well, for one, as a very, very serious author with many leather-bound books, it is imperative I start my books strong. Sadly, this is my best effort. Second, I want you to know I've loved and have been studying fantasy football for a long, long time. And finally, I think it's absolutely crucial to understand that, while there is certainly variance in fantasy sports, you are in control over your fate over the long run in DFS. If you are a long-term profitable player, you will make money playing this game if you don't completely screw up your bankroll management.

Instead of bitching about losing a game I was supposed to win, I should have been figuring out how I could have put myself in an even better position so I didn't have as much exposure to a down week as I did, which ultimately let me get beat by a worse squad. I should have been looking to improve instead of settling with just having the best team every single week of every single year and how in the shit did I lose to Brandon Jackson, Randy McMichael, and Mike Thomas!?

The lesson I learned is not only should I not try to avoid variance, but I should actually be embracing it. Shit happens. Sometimes you're handed pocket aces and sometimes you're dealt 2-7 off-suit; those fluctuations even out over time, but the manner in which you handle each of those scenarios will determine your fate as a daily fantasy player.

Much of this book is dedicated to learning how to cope with randomness, uncertainty, and luck. The data I provide is meant to put you in the best possible positions to land on the right side of variance, and the theories and strategies I propose are geared toward not only withstanding variance, but even benefiting from it. The thinking is that when things get crazy, we're going to make a lot of money.

My hope is this will lay the foundation for you to evolve as a daily fantasy player. Where you stand right now is less important than where you're headed, and I'm optimistic this book will give you the tools you need to constantly improve and adapt in the ever-changing daily fantasy market.

And if not, just send your seven-year-old brother a nasty email cussing him out for mistakes that were ultimately yours. It always goes over really, really well with family, and ultimately, what's the point of playing this crazy game if we can't ruin every meaningful relationship we have?

Jonathan Bales

Some Special Offers and Free Stuff

Let's just be honest. I give away free stuff in my books because it helps me make more money. But it's also good for you because...yeah, hi, free stuff. You give me your email, I give you something of value. Win-win.

For readers of this book, I have five special offers...

100% Bonus on DraftKings + Free Game

If you sign up and deposit on DraftKings, you'll immediately get a 100% deposit bonus up to $600. That's up to $600 for free just for signing up and depositing.

And use the promo code 'Bales' for free entry into a paid game.

Daily Fantasy Sports for Cash

★ ★ ★ ★ ★ EXCLUSIVE OFFER! ★ ★ ★ ★ ★

FREE ENTRY
TO A PAID GAME
WITH FIRST TIME DEPOSIT
★ ★ ★ ★ ★ ★ ★ ★ ★ ★ ★ ★ ★ ★ ★ ★
Use Promo Code BALES
www.DraftKings.com

Free Trial + 50% Off at Fantasy Labs

Fantasy Labs is my baby. If you don't already use it, you're absolutely going to love it. I teamed up with one of the best daily fantasy sports players in the world in CSURAM88, and we have an amazing development team. We've created a bunch of tools to help you win at DFS, the coolest of which is called Player Models—a simple-to-use tool that allows you to weigh all sorts of stats to create (and backtest) your own models, then optimize lineups off of your models. Even novice players can immediately create league-winning models, rankings, and lineups because we show you what actually works.

It's incredible, and I'm giving away a free trial and 50% off the first month. Just go to FantasyLabs.com and enter the code 'BALESBOOK' on the payment page to start your free trial.

A Free DFS Guide

I have a short e-book called *A Guide to Winning at Daily Fantasy Sports*. It contains some excerpts from other books and a bunch of new content as well. You can download it for free at http://eepurl.com/buuZWj.

10% Off Everything On My Site

If you want to purchase any of the other books in my Fantasy Sports for Smart People book series (or one of the other products I offer), you can do that at FantasyFootballDrafting.com. If you head over there, use the coupon code "Smart10" at checkout to get 10% off your entire order.

Free Course from RotoAcademy—My Daily Fantasy Training Marketplace

Finally, I'm giving away a free premium course from RotoAcademy. I teamed up with RotoGrinders to build RotoAcademy, which is a marketplace for premium DFS education. We sell entire courses, each made up of between four and 12 lessons designed to help you master a specific area of daily fantasy strategy. It's a fantastic way to supplement the data and advice you'll get from this book.

Head over to RotoGrinders.com/RotoAcademy to check it out. If you see a course you like, again, just email me at fantasyfootballdrafting@gmail.com (or tweet me @BalesFootball) and I'll send it to you for free.

A Daily Fantasy Sports Glossary

For the kids...

+EV

Positive Expected Value; a situation in which you expect a positive return on your investment. Daily fantasy players are constantly searching for +EV situations.

$/Point

Dollars per point; the number of dollars you must spend (in cap space) for every point a player is projected to score. A lower $/point is preferable.

50/50

A league type in which the top half of all entrants get paid and the bottom half lose their entry fee. 50/50 leagues are generally considered safe, but they can become dangerous if you enter the same lineup into multiple leagues.

Action

The amount of money you have in play

Bankroll

The amount of money you're willing to invest in daily fantasy sports

Barbara Walters Game

Courtesy of Al_Smizzle, a game/performance that was "obvious" with 20/20 hindsight

Bearish

A pessimistic outlook on a particular player, team, or situation. If you're bearish on a player, you wouldn't use him in your lineups.

Bullish

The opposite of bearish; an optimistic outlook on a particular situation. If you're bullish on a player, you'd use him in your daily fantasy lineups.

Buy-In

The amount of money needed to enter a particular league

Cash Game

Usually considered any league that pays out at least one-third of entrants (50/50s, heads-up games, and three-mans)

Ceiling

A player, team, or lineup's upside; the maximum number of points they could score

Chalk

The most obvious plays; the players who clearly offer a lot of value and will be highly owned

Commission

The fee charged by the daily fantasy sites to play in a league; typically around 10 percent of the total buy-ins

Confirmation Bias

The tendency to search for or confirm information that fits with preexisting beliefs

Contrarian

To go against the grain—the opposite of "chalk"

DFS

Acronym for daily fantasy sports

Donkey

A bad DFS player; someone who is -EV

Exposure

The amount of money invested in a player; if you have a lot of exposure to a particular player, it means you have a relatively high percentage of your bankroll placed on him.

Fade

To avoid a particular player or game, i.e. "I'm fading the Rockies game because I think the teams will be really highly owned."

Fish

The same thing as a donkey; a poor player

Floor

A player, team, or lineup's downside; the minimum number of points they could score

Freeroll

A daily fantasy league that's free to enter but has cash prizes

Game Flow

How a football game unfolds or is expected to unfold; helps predict opportunities

GOAT

Greatest of All-Time (in opposition to WOAT)

GPP

"Guaranteed Prize Pool"; a league in which the prize is guaranteed, regardless of the number of entrants

Head-to-head (Heads-Up)

A one-one-one daily fantasy league

Hedge

Actions taken to reduce the overall risk of your lineups; if you're excessively bullish on a particular lineup, for example, you would hedge by creating other lineups without any of the same players, even if it's sub-optimal. When you hedge, you're reducing risk at the cost of also reducing upside.

High-Low
Also known as "stars and scrubs"; when you select multiple elite, high-salary players to accompany low-priced, bargain bin players (in contrast to a balanced strategy)

Late Swap
To edit your lineup on DraftKings after a contest has started; you can edit players whose games have not yet begun

Lock
A must-play

Multiplier
A league in which you can multiply your entry fee by a certain factor based on the payouts; in a 5x multiplier, for example, the winners get paid out five times their entry fee. The higher the multiplier, the more high-risk/high-reward the league.

Narrative
A widely accepted explanation for a particular phenomenon, whether true or not; a "revenge game" is a type of narrative

Nuts
The best possible lineup; similar to "the nuts"—the best possible hand—in poker

Overlay
When a daily fantasy site loses money on a GPP; if $20,000 is guaranteed but there are only $18,000 worth of entrants, the overlay is $2,000.

Pivot
To move away from a player you previously had in your lineup; if you liked Troy Tulowitzki and he's scratched, you could pivot to a shortstop with a similar price tag.

Player Prop
A Vegas line that projects a particular stat for an individual player

Punt

A calculated, low-priced risk at a certain position used to save money elsewhere; if you go min-priced at second base, for example, you'd be punting the position so you can load up on studs. Punt plays lead to high-low lineup construction.

Qualifier

A league in which the winners don't receive cash, but rather win a "ticket" into another league; a 10-team qualifier with a $12 buy-in might give away one ticket into a larger league with a $100 buy-in, for example; in opposition to cash games

RBBC

Running Back By Committee; when an offense employs a timeshare at the running back position

Reach

To select a player who doesn't provide great value, i.e. a high $/point; reaches typically result in -EV (negative expected value) situations

Recency Bias

The tendency to place the most weight or have the easiest time remembering recent events/items in a series

ROI

Return on Investment

Shark

A really good DFS player

Splits

A player's stats in contrasting situations; ex: home/road splits

Stacking

To pair multiple players from the same professional team in an effort to increase upside; stacking is particularly popular in daily fantasy baseball

Sweat

Watching games with a lot on the line; ex: I was in first place in a huge GPP and sweating the final game of the night.

Tilting

To develop stress or anxiety from game outcomes that often leads to sub-optimal decision-making

Train

Entering the same lineup into one league multiple times (only advisable in qualifiers)

Vulture

When a fat running back steals a touchdown from the better player

Whale

A high-volume DFS player (whether good or bad)

"At the end of the day, you are solely responsible for your success and your failure. And the sooner you realize that, you accept that, and integrate that into your work ethic, you will start being successful. As long as you blame others for the reason you aren't where you want to be, you will always be a failure."

Erin Cummings

II. My Approach to Daily Fantasy ~~Football~~ Sports

"Markets are constantly in a state of uncertainty and flux and money is made by discounting the obvious and betting on the unexpected."

George Soros

I'm about to write a lot of words about my daily fantasy sports philosophy, all of which can be summarized in two: make money. I think pretty much everyone would say their goal is to make money, but, whether they know it or not, not everyone acts in a way that reflects that aim.

Before diving into this idea, I should perhaps talk briefly about where I see the daily fantasy sports industry heading. As DFS continues to grow exponentially—which I see happening fairly easily for at least the next year or two and potentially much longer—there will be more and more new players putting bad money into leagues. By 'bad money,' I mean they're probably –EV. The hope is that there's a "poker boom" sort of effect.

Well, most new players are attracted to tournaments, and because of that, I believe GPPs are going to become easier to beat in the coming years. I'm not sure exactly how I feel about cash games—head-to-heads in particular—but I do think those are easier to "solve" than tournaments. There might not be one truly optimal cash-game lineup, but there are certainly iterations that are closer to optimal than others. It's really easy for a profitable DFS player to scale his cash-game volume if he's winning such that it's possible most of the money in cash games (at least at higher stakes) is going to be "good money" and most of the money in GPPs will be "bad money."

That doesn't mean cash games can't be profitable. On the contrary, I think there's good evidence to suggest there are a handful of talented daily fantasy players making a shit ton of money in cash games. My buddy CSURAM88 is one of them.

The reason I don't see the long-term profitability in cash games improving in the same way as tournaments, however, is because GPPs represent more of a true marketplace in which there's massive upside in predicting and exploiting public opinion. That doesn't really exist in the same way in cash games—it's just optimal lineup versus optimal lineup— and at a certain point, you could make an argument that cash games will be solved.

Outside of minor exceptions, there's not really much game theory involved in cash games. Meanwhile, I think daily fantasy players are starting to realize more and more that the GPP landscape is governed almost entirely by game theory.

So What's Game Theory?

Game theory is basically the study of decision-making, specifically among competing (or cooperating) minds. When an offensive coordinator calls a run play on 3rd-and-7, he's (perhaps unknowingly) employing game theory, utilizing a play that's probably not optimal in a vacuum, but perhaps ideal after accounting for his opponent's thoughts and beliefs.

Here's another example of game theory that helps to demonstrate its effect on strategic decision-making in a competition. Let's say you're one of 1,000 people competing to guess the roll of a fair, six-sided die. You have to predict 10 rolls, guessing if each roll will land into one of two buckets: 1

& 2 or 3, 4, 5, & 6. There's no catch; there's indeed a 33% chance of a roll being a 1 or 2 and a 67% chance of it being 3, 4, 5, or 6.

If you weren't competing against anyone and simply asked to maximize the number of correct guesses, it's pretty clear you should select the second option every single time. Even though there will inevitably be rolls of 1 & 2, you're going to maximize your long-term accuracy by simply selecting the larger bucket of numbers on each roll.

But there are two different ways to act "optimally" in a zero-sum game. One is to simply try to maximize the number of points, or accuracy, or whatever it is. That's the easy part. The second way to act optimally is to maximize win probability. That's a lot more challenging when competing with others because everything they do well is a negative for you.

It should be pretty clear that the first version of "optimal" play wouldn't be optimal in our theoretical 1,000-man die-guessing league. Assuming the other 999 participants are rational, you can bet they're going to select the second bucket (with four numbers) over the first bucket (with two numbers) on most of the rolls. Some will probably select it on all 10 rolls.

Thus, the strategy that maximizes accuracy—selecting the second bucket on every roll—would actually be completely awful in practice; the only way you could win with that approach would be if not a single roll saw a 1 or 2 come up *and* all 999 other participants selected '1 & 2' at least once, i.e. absolutely terrible odds.

It should be pretty clear that, to win this game that I just realized is kind of confusing but I don't want to delete all of this and think of a new metaphor, you'd need to act in a "sub-optimal" way at least part of the time (that is, "sub-optimal" in terms of your long-term accuracy but hopefully optimal in terms of maximizing the chances of winning).

Game Theory, Public Psychology, and the GPP Marketplace

GPP success is a delicate balancing act. You're trying to balance player value—strict production minus cost—with public opinion.

In the die-rolling game, you probably wouldn't want to select '1 & 2' every single time because the odds of that happening would be quite small (1-in-54,049). So you want to be somewhere between one of the extremes in order to maximize the chances of beating everyone else. Where you fall on that spectrum is inherently tied to how others act. If you knew for a fact that none of your 999 opponents planned to select the second bucket on all 10 rolls, that would be the optimal choice for you. If you knew every single one planned to do it, the optimal choice for you would be to select that bucket nine times and the first bucket just once. Your chances of winning the competition would then be 33 percent—a remarkable percentage in a 1,000-person league—because you'd be even with them on every single roll except one.

This philosophy is exactly the same in tournaments. What's optimal is fundamentally tied to how you expect others to behave. If Peyton Manning is the top quarterback value and you expect him to be in 40 percent of lineups, while Tony Romo is the second-best value and you anticipate only 10 percent ownership, it should be pretty clear that Romo is the superior GPP play; he's the equivalent of selecting '1 & 2' when almost everyone else is on '3, 4, 5 & 6.' If you expected even ownership on the two players, Manning would become the best play (despite absolutely nothing changing in regards to what we typically consider his 'value'—namely, his cost and expected production).

More on Win Probability and Point-Maximization

DFS is my favorite game to play. I love it. But I like to play a lot of other games, too. I like poker, ping pong, darts, Stratego, Monopoly, foosball, and a bunch of weird games I made up and make my friends play. I even like Rock-Paper-Scissors and play it against a computer, like, every day. It's a great way to practice completely overthinking things.

One game I play all the time is called Fun Run. It's a mobile game and it's sort of like MarioKart in that you race and there are question mark things you can get that have weapons to kill your opponents (lightning, a bear trap thing, a sword, etc). I don't even really play video games at all but I really like this one because there's quite a bit of strategy involved.

When I first started playing, I just tried to move as fast as possible and finish the race with the quickest time I could. Seems logical...faster is better in any race, right? Maybe, maybe not. You need to perform well to win, but the goal of any race isn't to have the fastest time you can, but to have a faster time than everyone else. Those are similar ideas, but not exactly the same.

Thus, now my strategy is more about creating the largest possible difference between my time and that of my opponents. That might mean going out of my way to obtain an additional question mark, using a super low-variance strategy late in the race if I'm winning, taking more risks when I'm losing, and so on. In fact, the goal is almost never to minimize my time, but rather to maximize win probability.

Let me start a new paragraph and write that again: *the goal in any zero-sum game is to maximize win probability.*

This should sound familiar. While scoring a lot of points is a prerequisite for tournament success, your primary goal should not be point-maximization. It should be win-probability-maximization.

As I've mentioned, I think there are two layers of value in tournaments. There's the traditional dollar-per-point type of value—expected production minus cost—and then there's the usable value a player provides you. I think most players either overlook the second type of value completely or don't understand how important it really is.

In short, we need to be concerned not only with the chances of being right on a particular player, but also (perhaps more important) the benefits it actually provides us if we are indeed correct. What are the chances we hit on a pick *and* what's the payoff if that happens?

When you roster high-owned players, you're probably at least coming close to maximizing your point projection and the odds of your players "hitting." There's a reason they're highly owned; no one is in 30 percent of lineups if they're a shitty value. But in rostering the chalk in GPPs, we're also minimizing the potential payoff. If you hit on a quarterback who is in 33 percent of lineups, you're still completely even with one-third of the field. If you hit on one in five percent of lineups, you have a leg up on 95 percent of users.

Another way to look at this idea is to consider situations in which you've been trailing in a tournament. When you're in, say, 50th place in a big GPP with two players remaining, it certainly feels a whole lot better if those guys aren't in lineups ahead of you, right? If there are multiple lineups ahead of you with the same players left to go, you have no shot at winning. At that point, you'd certainly trade in those two players for a pair that is unique and gives you a shot at the win, even if they're slightly less valuable, right? Of course.

Being contrarian leads to less fantasy scoring over the long run, but it also gives you more "outs," so to speak, in the event that you need to jump other users (which happens almost all the time in a GPP). If pulled off correctly, it can maximize your win probability without maximizing points. In my opinion, it is a forward-looking DFS strategy that acknowledges fallibility—as opposed to a shortsighted "I'm going to take the best values because I want to score as many points as possible (and it couldn't possibly be the case that I'm wrong about these guys or even that I'm right and they don't work out)."

By going against the grain, you're leaving yourself room for measurement errors, which is basically what my entire DFS strategy is about. I know it's challenging to predict fantasy scoring, even in predictable sports, and it's even more difficult to beat an entire field of really smart people. So for the most part, I'd rather focus on maximizing the benefit I receive if everyone else is wrong. I don't need to be better than everyone else when it comes to projecting players; I just need to have a comparable level of predictive ability in that area if I'm putting myself in a better position when it comes to reaping the fruits of my labor. In being contrarian, I'm betting on low-frequency events that have asymmetrical payoffs such that, although I'm going to be wrong more than I'm right, I'm going to be overcompensated for being right when that happens.

There are times when we can have our cake and eat it too, acquiring high-value players who are also low-usage. In fact, I'd never recommend being contrarian just for the sake of it, picking off-the-map players with no rhyme or reason. However, the overarching idea is that we need to balance value with ownership, using game theory to determine which players provide not only the greatest traditional value in terms of dollars-per-point, but also those that offer maximum usable value in terms of increasing the odds of winning.

In short, others' decisions in a marketplace setting are arguably the most important components in determining what's optimal for you.

A brief aside: I was watching the World Series of Poker yesterday and I thought of another good example to add here that I think displays the power of "uniqueness" in poker, and indirectly DFS. You're in a poker tournament and two players ahead of you go all-in. You call, putting all of their chips at risk. The others both flip over Ace-Queen. Which hand would you prefer: King-Queen or King-Jack?

It's obviously the latter, even though it is theoretically the weaker hand. It keeps you alive, giving you outs and a much higher chance of winning the hand. Actually, because the duo ahead of you has the same hand, you'd basically be competing heads-up in order to triple-up (or triple the largest of their chip stacks, anyway)—great odds if you can get them—but it works only if your opponents have the same hand and you have two live cards.

The same is true in daily fantasy; the more common your opponents' lineups and the more yours is differentiated, the better your odds, all else equal.

Further, you know King-Jack is suitable to King-Queen only after you have knowledge of the opponents' hands. Prior to the hand, you'd very clearly prefer King-Queen. The difference between poker and DFS is we can "know" our opponents' cards before the hand is dealt; because we're dealing with a large sample size of lineups in a GPP, the individual lineup fluctuations even out and we can very often forecast player ownership such that, if played properly, we can predict our opponents' hands and play not necessarily the one that's most optimal in a vacuum, but the one that's most capable of "filling in the gaps" to beat our opponents.

Also, why the fuck did you call two all-in raises with King-Queen anyway bro?

Predictability and Being Contrarian

One difference between daily fantasy sports and the die-rolling game is that, in the latter, we know the probability of at least one variable, i.e. the roll of the die. In both contests, we need to predict 1) expected performance and 2) public perception of expected performance. A player (or a number on a die) is a good play if the former exceeds the latter.

With the die, there's a 33 percent chance of rolling a 1 or 2. If you were betting on the rolls, you'd need better than 2-to-1 odds to make betting on 1 or 2 a +EV decision. That's because the odds of a different number coming up are twice as great as 1 or 2.

In daily fantasy sports tournaments, ownership represents odds. With Manning and Romo at 40 and 10 percent ownership, respectively, you're getting incredible odds to "bet" on Romo, even though he's the worse value in terms of expected production and cost.

A hidden assumption of all this, however—and I think the best argument against the contrarian movement—is that predicting player ownership is very difficult. I'm going to do my best to provide some data and tips to help predict ownership later in this book, but I do think it's a somewhat valid criticism. If we can't predict ownership with any sort of accuracy, then there's no sense in fading high-value players.

My rebuttal (to my own criticism) is that predicting player production is really challenging, too. And I think it's arguably more difficult to predict how players will perform, especially in sports like baseball and football, than it is to determine who other people like. For the most part, we know when certain players are going to have ownership that's really high. But go ahead and try to predict the top five fantasy scorers in a given week of NFL for me and let me know how that goes.

This all comes down to my belief that the more randomness there is in a sport, the more value there is in using low-owned players—the more value there is in going against the grain and being contrarian. That's why I think your approach to a game like daily fantasy basketball should be much different than that in one like baseball. The former is fairly predictable night to night, and thus it's extremely risky to fade an obvious star value. LeBron James is never going to go 0-for-4 with three strikeouts. Mainly because he plays a different sport, but also because, you know, variance and stuff.

Football falls in between baseball and basketball on the predictability spectrum—not completely random by any means, but certainly still a challenge to accurately predict on a weekly basis. But here's the thing: people still act as though they have a ton of confidence in their selections. If we want expected production to exceed public perception of production but obvious values are widely utilized by the public, you can make an argument that top values are never quality GPP plays (certainly not batters in baseball, whose production is extremely volatile, yet often still see 30+ percent ownership).

In effect, you can think of GPP strategy as playing poker and going all-in on various hands. You can choose to go all-in with the nuts hand—pocket aces—but with really poor odds. Or you can choose a worse hand with awesome odds—odds that make the strategy more long-term profitable than choosing aces.

Tournament ownership is equivalent to those odds. And until the market adjusts appropriately, there's going to be a lot of meat left on the bone when it comes to selecting "sub-optimal" values. That doesn't mean we can just play anyone, but rather the goal is to take a "best-of-the-rest" approach, forgoing just a little bit of value in order to get dramatically reduced ownership, i.e. significantly better odds to play only a slightly worse hand.

Why GPPs Are Very Beatable

My approach to tournaments is admittedly volatile. Since I'm generally playing under-the-radar teams and offenses that are rarely the top values or highest-owned guys, I usually do either very well or very poorly. I can pass a lot of lineups in a hurry at times, but also fall very quickly if the chalk does well. That's sort of the point, though; I embrace that volatility in GPPs. I've tracked my DFS results since I began employing a truly contrarian GPP approach, and I finish in the top 10 percent *and* bottom 10 percent of tournaments around twice as much as you'd expect from chance alone. That would be horrible in a 50/50, but it's ideal in a tournament.

My strategy definitely doesn't maximize point-scoring and it probably doesn't maximize my rate of cashes, either. I think that's actually why tournaments are beatable and will be for a long time; users act in a way that represents what they believe to be their personal best interest—maximizing points and the probability of cashing—and that results in the chalk being over-owned and certain contrarian selections being under-owned.

Even when people think they're being contrarian, they probably aren't most of the time. Everyone sort of thinks and acts in the same way. We all have access to more or less the same information and most of us process it in similar ways.

We all suffer from the same biases. We all naturally want exposure to the top plays and we all naturally fear doing something that we know limits our chances of cashing.

The result is that long-tail events aren't fully accounted for in ownership. The GPP landscape is going to continue to shift dramatically, but I believe it's going to be very difficult even for rational individuals—all acting in their own self-interest—to find and maintain the perfect balance between probability and ownership such that there aren't major inefficiencies in tournaments. Maybe that will happen one day, but I don't think it's going to be soon. That doesn't mean there are everlasting holes we will always be able to exploit—just that competing individuals will have a difficult time finding the production/ownership equilibrium when the GPP meta game is so complex; when the herd figures out the "right" strategy, it's no longer right.

Antifragility in DFS

In my last book on daily fantasy baseball, I proposed the idea of using an antifragile tournament philosophy. Antifragility is a term coined by the great Nassim Nicholas Taleb—a writer, investor, and epistemologist who made killings in the 1987, 2000, and 2008 financial crises. His investment strategy is based upon "black swans"—rare and unpredictable events that humans tend to dismiss as outliers after the fact.

Basically, antifragility is the ability to benefit from chaos or volatility. As Taleb explains:

> *Some things benefit from shocks: they thrive and grow when exposed to volatility, randomness, disorder, and stressors and love adventure, risk, and uncertainty. Yet, in spite of the ubiquity of the*

phenomenon, there is no word for the exact opposite of fragile. Let us call it antifragile.

Antifragility is beyond resilience or robustness. The resilient resists shocks and stays the same; the antifragile gets better. This property is behind everything that has changed with time: evolution, culture, ideas, revolutions, political systems, technological innovation, cultural and economic success, corporate survival, good recipes (say, chicken soup or steak tartare with a drop of cognac), the rise of cities, cultures, legal systems, equatorial forests, bacterial resistance. Even our own existence as a species on this planet. And antifragility determines the boundary between what is living and organic (or complex), say, the human body, and what is inert, say, a physical object like the stapler on your desk.

The antifragile loves randomness and uncertainty, which also means – crucially – a love of errors, a certain class of errors. Antifragility has a singular property of allowing us to deal with the unknown, to do things without understanding them - and do them well. Let me be more aggressive: we are largely better at doing than we are at thinking, thanks to antifragility. I'd rather be dumb and antifragile than extremely smart and fragile, any time.

I think that last sentence is one of my favorite of Taleb's, and also one I believe is incredibly applicable to daily fantasy sports. There are a lot of smart people playing this game. A lot of dumb ones, too, but still some smarty-pants. I don't want to compete with those guys. I'd rather admit that I don't know all that much—concede that forecasting sports outcomes is more challenging than what I naturally want to believe—and then use that lack of predictability to my advantage, making money when others are wrong. You could play a 100-man tournament against 99 of the top DFS players in the world and, if they're all smart enough to identify and play the top values, you can sure make a lot of money capitalizing on that lineup overlap and benefiting when things don't work out their way. That's basically what I believe is happening in the tournament ecosystem right now, especially at high stakes: very smart players acting in a way that rewards antifragility.

Antifragility isn't always ideal in life or in daily fantasy sports. Taleb classifies things into one of three categories: fragile, robust, and antifragile. A mirror is fragile; it is harmed by fragility and doesn't deal well with stressors. We never really want fragility in our DFS lineups.

A diamond is an example of something that's robust, or resilient. It doesn't benefit from chaos—a diamond doesn't get better when you drop it, for example—but it isn't hurt, either. It's basically indifferent to uncertainty and chaos.

For so long, these two labels were all we had. The opposite of something that's harmed by volatility is something that isn't harmed by volatility, right? Well, Taleb opened our eyes to antifragility. Evolution is antifragile. Not only is it not hurt by chaos—by errors—but it thrives and exists *because* of randomness. Indeed, we exist and can play this amazing game of DFS because of a series of random mutations.

Or, if you're reading this in rural Alabama, we exist and can play this amazing game of DFS because...Jesus.

Viruses and bacteria are other examples of something antifragile. There's a reason your doctor tells you to continue taking antibiotics even after you feel well. Bacteria are capable of surviving and thriving in the face of adversity, coming back even stronger after a shortened dose of antibiotics. They become more difficult to kill after being exposed to stress.

To give you an idea of how this applies to DFS, I brainstormed some types of lineups that could fit into each Taleb category.

Fragile: Wide range of outcomes in cash games

In cash games, your primary goal is consistently scoring above the mean. I do actually think there's more of a difference between 50/50s and head-to-head games than people think; in the former, you can't get beat by outliers like you can in the latter. I also think there's merit to point-maximization and seeking pure value in head-to-head games, while 50/50s are all about (or mostly, anyway) improving your lineup's floor.

Still, one of the aims in all cash games is to limit the range of outcomes for your team. If the cashing line in a 50/50 is 120 points, it's better to score 125 points two-thirds of the time than to sometimes score 180 points and sometimes score 90 points, even if the latter range of outcomes results in a higher average score.

The way to narrow the range of outcomes in cash games is to 1) pay for the most consistent positions and 2) avoid high-variance players. In daily fantasy football, this typically means spending (and even overspending) on an elite quarterback (and often running back, too), finding value at the volatile pass-catching positions, and jumping on players whose production isn't very dependent on a particular game script.

For example, Jeremy Hill is an example of a running back who isn't at all ideal for cash games. He doesn't catch a lot of passes and he's very touchdown-dependent, which widens his range of outcomes in each game. If the Bengals get down early, Hill can be rendered almost useless. His week-to-week outlook, even if he offers value, is fragile.

Fragile Cash Lineup: Cheap quarterback, running backs dependent on a particular game script, pass-catchers who see a lot of deep targets, players who rely heavily on touchdowns over receptions

Robust: Narrow range of outcomes in cash games

Compare Hill to a player like Matt Forte, whose pass-catching ability means he's still productive even if things don't go according to plan early in games for Chicago; Forte is robust in that his production comes almost independently of game flow. Those types of players—along with receivers who see a lot of high-percentage short targets, like Julian Edelman—are outstanding for cash games, especially in a full PPR site like DraftKings.

By rostering players like Forte and Edelman, you're trading in point-maximization (at times) for more exposure to a predictable range of outcomes.

Robust Cash Lineup: Elite quarterback, running backs who thrive regardless of the game flow, pass-catchers who see an abundance of screens and other short targets, players who rely on volume over touchdowns

Antifragile: Wide range of outcomes, low ownership in tournaments

In cash games, there's not much incentive to predict public opinion. Even if you know beyond a shadow of a doubt your head-to-head opponent is going to roster Tom Brady, it still might be the right decision for you to do that, too, if he's the clear-cut best value.

In tournaments, though, exploiting public perception is how we can become antifragile. Again, this all comes down to ownership levels being too high on certain players, creating an asymmetric payoff that rewards contrarian thinkers.

Antifragile GPP Lineup: Quarterback (sometimes cheap) stacked with at least one pass-catcher on his team, elite wide receivers (sometimes even slightly overpriced), elite tight end, players capable of realistically scoring two touchdowns, complete fade of most players with high projected ownership (cheap running backs with probable heavy workloads being the exception)

Why Being Contrarian Works

Being contrarian works because of others' overconfidence in their beliefs. Taleb has an awesome example of how manufactured stability leads to overconfidence.

> *A turkey is fed for a thousand days by a butcher; every day confirms to its staff of analysts that butchers love turkeys 'with increased statistical confidence.' The butcher will keep feeding the turkey until a few days before Thanksgiving. Then comes the day when it is really not a very good idea to be a turkey. So with the butcher surprising it, the turkey will have a revision of belief – right when its confidence in the statement the butcher loves turkeys is maximal and 'it is very quiet' and soothingly predictable in the life of the turkey.*

> *The example builds on the adaptation of a metaphor by Bertrand Russell. The key here is that such a surprise will be a Black Swan event; but just for the turkey, not for the butcher. We can also see from the turkey story the mother of all harmful mistakes: mistaking absence of evidence (of harm) for evidence of absence, a mistake that we will see tends to*

prevail in intellectual circles and one that is grounded in the social sciences. So our mission in life becomes simply 'how not to be a turkey,' or, if possible, how to be a turkey in reverse – antifragile, that is. 'Not being a turkey' starts with figuring out the difference between true and manufactured stability.

Football is the ultimate sport to buck conventional wisdom because it is so narrative-driven. There are a variety of reasons for this. One is that there is a week between games and we need something to talk about. There's a whole lot of time to overanalyze a single performance.

Another major reason for our dearth of understanding of the NFL is the lack of games in general. Imagine drawing conclusions about a baseball player after 16 games—less than 10 percent of the season. That would be ludicrous, yet I know that I've personally declared that a rookie "sucks ass" after like four games.

The narratives we create are ultimately widely accepted and fuel public opinion, which obviously has a massive impact on tournament ownership. When a rookie has three awesome games in a row, he's a stud and the most consistent player in the world and an obvious value. Or it could be the case that he's the turkey and in for a surprise.

Again, this all comes down to how public perception matches up with reality, and the lack of predictability in the NFL means high-value players are overcompensated for in GPPs. That lack of week-to-week consistency, working in conjunction with limited data to which we have access and a changing NFL landscape, means the public places way too much confidence in consensus narratives (even if they're true). And the more "obvious" the answer and the more people that buy in, the greater the rewards we can reap when the turkey finds out it's Thanksgiving.

Being contrarian works because narratives create a false level of confidence that artificially inflates ownership on certain players, producing a payoff for going against the grain that significantly exceeds the risk.

Predicting Ownership

In the same way the value of our projections extends only insofar as the level of confidence we can hold in their accuracy, the value of being contrarian—or antifragile—extends only insofar as we can predict ownership. And predicting ownership is difficult, but I think it can be done with some level of precision—at least as much as we have projecting player performances.

I'm going to discuss some more micro-level predictors of ownership later in the book, but I also wanted to run over some of the more philosophical macro items that I believe affect player and team popularity in GPPs.

Competition (Buy-In Level)

A contrarian approach to daily fantasy sports is based around the assumption that we're going to profit from inefficiencies in the ways other people behave. The backbone of being contrarian, then, is knowing your opponents. How are they going to choose players in specific situations? How price-sensitive will they be? When do they like to fade the chalk?

The level of competition you're facing—of which the buy-in level is a decent proxy—can tell you a lot about how your competition is going to act. I wrote down some thoughts about this at RotoGrinders last year.

> *Odell Beckham Jr. has absolutely dominated in his rookie year – far more so than I imagined he would*

*in any season – and he was present in all
three DraftKings championship lineups in Week 16
(Flea Flicker, Chop Block, and Main Event).*

*What was really interesting to me wasn't that
Beckham was in all three lineups, but rather the
varying levels of usage in each: 3.3 percent in the
Main Event, 6.5 percent in the Chop Block, and 9.3
percent in the Flea Flicker. That's nearly twice as
much usage in the Chop Block and three times as
much in the Flea Flicker as compared to the Main
Event.*

*If you recall, the Main Event was a $1,500 buy-in, the
Chop Block was just $50, and the Flea Flicker was $5.
I don't think I'm going out on a limb in saying that,
overall, the level of competition is stiffer in leagues
with higher buy-ins. There are lots of –EV players at
all levels, but you aren't going to run into any John-
Kuhn-led lineups in a league that costs $1,500 to
enter.*

Skill Level and Price Sensitivity

*Last week, Beckham was the most expensive wide
receiver on DraftKings and he was facing a pretty hot
St. Louis Rams defense. Beckham absolutely torched
them, but I'd argue that he wasn't the best value at
the wide receiver position.*

*The fact that Beckham's usage was so low in the
Main Event confirms that idea. Just 1-in-30 rosters
were led by Beckham, suggesting that the "sharp"
money was on other guys. That doesn't mean
Beckham was a poor play, but just that he was*

probably overpriced, regardless of how well he ended up playing.

It's always difficult to come to a consensus on value, but I've noticed that same trend in price-sensitivity all season; DraftKings users in lower buy-ins care less about price and more about recent performance and expected production. Whereas smart daily fantasy users are generally trying to balance value with expected ownership in GPPs, novice users typically aren't extremely value-focused.

Being Contrarian Based on League Type
I think game theory is a major component of tournament success, and the best players are typically thinking one step ahead of their opponents. We're basically playing a more complicated version of rock-paper-scissors.

That means that what is "optimal" in tournaments depends on what your opponents are doing. And based on (admittedly anecdotal) evidence this year, I believe that we should approach low and medium-stakes GPPs differently than higher buy-ins.

Specifically, winning cheaper tournaments is probably more about finding value – somewhat similar to our strategy in cash games – because 1) it's more difficult to predict usage and 2) we can sometimes combine value and low ownership because most users don't care about maximizing overall value. Ideally, we want both high-value players and a unique tournament lineup – something that's workable in cheaper tourneys.

The problem with a value-based approach at higher stakes is that there isn't as much "bad" money on low-value players. The players who offer value are typically in a lot of lineups, so it's sometimes quite difficult to have a ton of value and still find low-ownership players.

For that reason, I believe it makes more sense to go against the grain against better players. The idea is that all of the usable value from "high-value" players dissipates since their usage is typically so high. The potential similarity of lineups in high-stakes leagues adds more actual value (the pragmatic kind) to forgoing player value (the theoretical kind) in terms of expected production and price.

In short: be price-sensitive when others aren't, and be contrarian when others are too price-sensitive.

In the case of Beckham, I personally would have 100 percent rostered him if I knew he'd have just 3.3 percent usage in the Main Event, but I would have never rostered him at the nearly 10 percent usage he saw in cheaper leagues.

Same player, same price, different decision based on the thoughts and actions of others. That approach, in my view, is the easiest way to find success against the crowd in large-field leagues.

I'm going to be doing a lot more research in this area, but it's pretty obvious that there's a greater level of price-sensitivity at higher stakes. That's especially true with daily fantasy football, which is the primary means of customer acquisition for DFS sites. There are so many new players coming into the industry—so much bad money—that value probably is only a relatively small part of ownership. I'd argue new players care more about rostering hot players than getting guys at the right prices.

That means there could potentially be meat left on the bone to roster high-value players in low and medium-stakes GPPs. However, that could be changing. It is becoming easier and easier for new users to field quality DFS lineups; there are more sites than ever out there. You can take a quick look at Fantasy Labs to get a general sense of which players offer value in a given week. Even just comparing rankings from a few different sites and playing the guys who are continually at the top is a decent way to find a wisdom-of-the-crowd source of player value.

While I'm certainly more price-sensitive in low-stakes GPPs and more contrarian at higher stakes, I do think the competition will stiffen such that there will be greater selection accuracy at lower stakes in the future.

And again, I think that actually makes tournaments *more* beatable. To maximize the extent from which we can benefit from chaos—from the crowd being wrong—we need as much lineup overlap as possible. The more groupthink and the more users care about production minus cost, the more incentive there is to fade high-value players.

The overarching idea here is that your lineup creation should be dictated not only by league type, but also by your competition; you can't properly exploit inefficiencies if you can't predict how they'll act.

Multi-Entry

Ahh, the great multi-entry debate. I'm not really going to get into the pros and cons of multi-entry tournaments. Actually nevermind, yes I will.

In my view, multi-entry tournaments fuel the DFS industry. If you want to be able to win $1 million on a $20 entry or $100,000 on a $3 lineup, then you like multi-entry. Tournaments that allow unlimited entries (or a very high number of them) bring in so much cash, and that cash is reinvested into customer acquisition and the giant prize pools you see today. If it weren't for the guys who enter a crapload of lineups into a single league, regular Joes wouldn't be able to get rich in one day of fantasy sports without a huge investment.

Further, the argument that users can completely cover their bases, playing every iteration of a lineup and basically guaranteeing a win, is completely flawed. There are billions of possible lineup variations such that ensuring a win—or even anything close to it—is impossible.

Plus, multi-entry users have one of two choices when creating their lineups: diversify a whole lot to ensure a floor on their return, or don't diversify much. In the former, they're necessarily playing sub-optimal values, which can be a positive for the average user. In the latter, they're taking on a huge amount of risk, which I believe is overlooked by most casual users. Yes, a guy with 100 lineups has a better chance to win than one with one lineup—but he also invested 100 times the money. The question is if his chances of winning are significantly more than 100 times greater *because* he has additional entries, and I don't think that's the case; rather, I believe the proportional win percentages are governed mostly by the relative skill levels of the competitors.

Whatever. What I really want to talk about is how our strategy should change in a multi-entry tournament versus a single-entry one, because I do think there are some differences here. Specifically, it makes more sense to be ultra-contrarian in a single-entry league, while multi-entry, especially in football, is more about balancing ownership and value.

The reason I believe this to be the case and have experienced success employing this approach is because single-entry tournaments generally contain a higher percentage of chalk. With just one entry, most users want to give it their best shot. They're generally stacking the Rockies when they're at home or playing Peyton Manning and Demaryius Thomas against the Raiders on primetime TV.

In multi-entry tournaments, however, you have users who are diversifying quite a bit. Not everyone does that—there are some really awesome players who create dozens of lineups without using more than a handful of players—but most multi-entry players want exposure to a wider range of players. That reduces ownership on chalk, increases it on less valuable players, and enhances the worth of a value-based approach over a contrarian.

Don't get me wrong; I still believe there's massive value in taking an antifragile approach to multi-entry tournaments, too, but it's heightened in single-entry GPPs. Those formats create more lineup overlap, which is the antifragile DFS player's best friend. We *want* it to be easy to identify values and we *want* there to be an incentive to use those guys.

But again, this all comes down to predicting others' behavior and utilizing the strategy most likely to capitalize on potential inefficiencies.

Predictability

I started playing a little daily fantasy basketball this past year. I won a bunch of money in the first tournament I ever played. I lost it all back very quickly. I'm really just not very good at daily fantasy basketball.

Turns out it helps to know something about the sport. So that's one reason I failed. Another is that basketball is not at all conducive to my style of play because, as I mentioned earlier, it's incredibly predictable on a nightly basis relative to baseball and football.

There was one point last year when Russell Westbrook was going absolutely nuts every night and was a very clear value. He was 80 percent owned in tournaments, and you still couldn't fade him because there was like a 90 percent chance he was gonna score 60 or 70 points on DraftKings. You're kind of handcuffed in that way; there's some incentive to go against the grain at times, I'm sure—it could be that I just have no idea when the hell to do that—but it's just really difficult to fade the chalk, even at ridiculous ownership percentages, because of the predictability of the sport.

Football isn't like basketball in terms of game-to-game predictability. It's very much an event-based sport like baseball; one wind gust or a single shoestring tackle can totally alter a player's fantasy impact. Because of that, there's what I believe to be over-usage on the top values. The fact that we can't be extremely confident in our player rankings and projections should be reflected in ownership, but it isn't. Instead, we often see something like this:

Peyton Manning: 12% chance of being top quarterback, 30% ownership

Drew Brees: 11% chance of being top quarterback, 20% ownership

Tom Brady: 10% chance of being top quarterback, 15% ownership

Aaron Rodgers: 9% chance of being top quarterback, 9% ownership

Tony Romo: 8% chance of being top quarterback, 5% ownership

For the sake of argument, we'll just say all of these players offer the exact same value in terms of cost and expected production. In this instance, Manning would be the top signal-caller, but he'd also offer the least usable tournament value due to being over-utilized; you aren't getting the right odds to "call" on him, so to speak.

Meanwhile, Romo offers a slightly reduced probability of going off—33% lower than Manning—but his ownership is just 16.7% of Manning's. Romo would be the superior tournament play. Further, we could change absolutely nothing about the players' pricing or projections and Manning might become the top play if his ownership were lower; public perception drives usable tournament value.

This all comes back to the consistency and predictability of specific players and positions. Quarterback is the most predictable position on a weekly basis—and thus it's the spot at which I'm least likely to be contrarian because we know ownership rates will be higher—and yet we still see more usable value on lower-value players, in my opinion, due to public overconfidence about who the "best" plays are.

Wide receiver is a far more volatile position, and thus it is one of my favorite to go against the grain. I think one of the most underrated strategies is to "overpay" for stud receivers to get reduced ownership. When Demaryius Thomas is $9,000 in a difficult matchup and Antonio Brown is $8,700 in a juicy one, I know Brown is going to be more heavily utilized. I have no problem paying the extra $300 to get a player like Thomas who can go for 200/2 in any game. That variance surrounding wide receiver performances is a crucial factor in determining how aggressive you want to be in fading the chalk.

Dealing in Probabilities

Naturally, I think most people generally understand there aren't "locks" and each player has a certain probability of performing well in a given game. Whether or not that performance is actually uncertain or determined beforehand is a philosophical discussion I would love to write about—look out for my next book on the relationship between free will, determinism, and quantum mechanics—but I actually don't think it really matters for us; even if things were determined beforehand, we still need to be worried about the probability of us correctly predicting the future with the information we have at our disposal.

Nonetheless, I don't think the general public typically acts in a way that reflects the uncertainty we should have about game outcomes. This is of course the philosophy behind a contrarian strategy. But it should also affect everything from bankroll management to player evaluation to lineup creation.

Concerning the latter, I think football in particular is a sport in which we need to get away from the traditional median projections and dollar-per-point philosophies and instead visualize performances as a range of potential outcomes. Here's an example of what I mean...

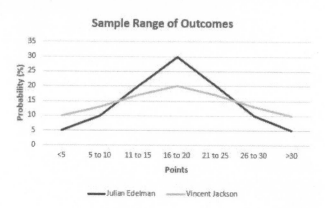

This is a sample scoring probability distribution for two very different players in Julian Edelman and Vincent Jackson. I have a lot more data coming on how to dissect player and position variance, but players like Edelman have proven to be very consistent in the past, while those similar to Jackson have displayed a large amount of weekly volatility.

Anyway, it doesn't really matter. The point is that we could have two players projected exactly the same (a median projection of 18 points for both Edelman and Jackson in this case), and yet their range of outcomes might look completely different. In this case, Edelman has a much narrower range of outcomes with a higher floor, but a lower ceiling.

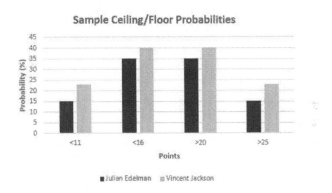

This shows the probability of each player performing at the tail ends of their scoring likelihood, and you can see Jackson is more likely to hit each level—nearly a coin flip to score either fewer than 11 points or more than 25 points, compared to just a 30 percent chance of Edelman doing that. Simply put, Jackson can be expected to have much more extreme results than Edelman on a weekly basis. Sometimes he will have two catches for 20 yards, sometimes seven catches for 150 yards and two scores.

That volatility doesn't make Jackson a worse play than Edelman—just a different one. I think it's so important to realize the difference between these two types of players because daily fantasy football is, for the most part, a game of either increasing upside or minimizing downside.

In cash games (especially 50/50s), you benefit from narrowing your lineup's range of outcomes. Let me give an example of why this is the case. Compare two players, one who (somehow, for the sake of this ridiculous example) scores 130 points with every single lineup, and one who averages the same score of 130 points by reaching 100 points half the time and 160 points the other half.

If those two players were competing in 50/50s with an average cash line of, say, 120 points, the former would win almost all the time by minimizing his range of outcomes and the latter would win only half the time (and lose money to rake) by widening his range of outcomes. Same projection, completely different results.

Now let's place those two players in GPPs in which the min-cash line is around 150 points. The former would never cash while the latter would cash half the time—a very high rate for GPPs. Things aren't this binary in reality, but you get the point; there's massive value in matching certain player types with particular DFS leagues to make sure you're giving yourself max exposure to favorable outcomes.

If there's a league in which a median projection can make some sense, I think it's probably head-to-head games (where, unlike a 50/50, you can get beat by outliers). Still, given the choice between a narrow or wide range of outcomes in a head-to-head contest, I'm taking the former. I might not be as likely to trade in a few projected points for safety like I would in a 50/50, but I'm definitely unlikely to use a player like Vincent Jackson in any type of cash game unless he's an insane value.

All of this has led me personally to spend a lot of time of late focusing on probabilities to better predict player volatility and exactly how much exposure guys have to certain outcomes. Okay, Rob Gronkowski has a median projection of 20 points this week, but what's the probability he tanks? Should I be spending that much on a tight end in a cash game, even if he offers decent dollar-per-point value?

These are questions we're trying to answer at Fantasy Labs. Our NFL product deals with probabilities, projecting ranges for each player using historic predictors of volatility. For running backs, we're looking at things like pass-catching ability, the Vegas lines, projected game flow, weather, and so on. You'll find a pass-catching running back is far less volatile than, say, a one-dimensional back on a team projected to lose by four points.

There's massive value in this manner of evaluation, too. It's not that median projections are useless—I still do them myself—but just that the daily fantasy industry as a whole is getting smarter. It's easier than ever to find quality projections and rankings, so we all have a decent idea that a good projection for Gronk in a given week might be somewhere between 16 and 18 points, for example.

However, there isn't nearly as much focus on probability distributions and using league types and payout structures to dictate player evaluation, i.e. there's a big potential edge if you can properly predict player floors and ceilings.

Player Comps

BeepImaJeep is one of my favorite daily fantasy sports players. He's also one of the best in the world, utilizing a game-theory-based approach very similar to mine to win tournaments. What's really interesting about BeepImaJeep is that, until recently, he really didn't know too much about sports (mainly because he's not a sports fan). He uses math to exploit inefficiencies in public opinion.

When asked how he can be so successful despite not enjoying (or watching) sports, BeepImaJeep argued that the best Scrabble players in the world don't know English. They utilize general heuristics to memorize words, and because they can't speak the language, they don't develop as many biases toward certain words as we might. They can basically play in a manner that's uninhibited; their lack of knowledge is a strength.

It's a really interesting analogy, and one I think is really relevant to daily fantasy football, in particular. I can't tell you how many times I've come to the conclusion I should start a specific player and then said, "Nah, I can't start that guy in this situation," only to see him blow up. What I thought I knew about a player's limitations was probably incorrect or at least somewhat flawed. And in a marketplace like daily fantasy tournaments in which there are huge benefits in thinking differently, it was really shortsighted of me to not do a better job of trying to overcome my initial biases. It's really difficult to not be swayed by the herd.

I bring this up because one of the ways I think we can at least partially overcome the groupthink that dominates NFL analysis is by sorting similar players into buckets—creating player comps. This is something a site called RotoViz already does, looking at how similar players have performed against comparable defenses in the past.

There are two major advantages to this form of analysis, I think. The first is getting away from the natural biases that inevitably plague our thinking. I always find it funny when I read former NFL scouts' evaluations of incoming rookies in which they generally provide a comp for each prospect. The comps are inevitably players who are superficially similar to the rookie in question; I can't tell you how many times I've seen a scout compare a rookie to an NFL player who went to the same school as him. How amazing is it that all of these rookies are just like NFL stars who attended the same school? Or how about how every white player's closest comp is…yup, another white player. Julian Edelman *must be* just like Wes Welker, right?

The second advantage afforded by player comps is assessing players in a probabilistic manner. When you compare one player to, say, 20 others, you obtain a natural range of outcomes—real past results—that can aid in estimating a player's probability of scoring X fantasy points.

This form of analysis is exactly what we're doing at Fantasy Labs, projecting players' ceilings and floors based on a variety of relevant factors (and allowing you to build and test models around the data). So if we want to project Julian Edelman against the Dolphins, we might look at how players similar to Edelman (those who play in the slot, see short targets, receive X red zone targets per game, etc) perform against defenses similar to Miami's (similar pass rush and secondary, for example) in comparable games (Team X projected by Vegas to win by Y points). Then we can provide each player with a volatility score to help determine his risk and upside in a given game.

The reason we use this form of analysis over, say, just looking at a player's past results, is because there's just so much variance in the NFL. A player like Vincent Jackson could come into the NFL and perform very consistently over the course of a season or two just by dumb luck. Examining the sorts of targets Jackson receives, we know he's going to be an extremely volatile receiver; because of the noise in football stats over small samples, we're better off "trading in" a bit of relevancy (as in studying players *similar* to Jackson) in favor of much larger sample sizes.

This is similar to predicting injuries by looking at physical predictors in addition to past injuries. It's not that past injuries contain no relevant information—they do—but there's so much noise in injuries since they're relatively random that we need to consider other variables. In doing that, we can know a lean 6'1'' running back coming off a torn hamstring is much more likely to get injured again than a stout 5'9'' running back (body-mass index is a major predictor of injury rates).

Correlational Effects

So we're trying to construct teams that give us the most exposure to specific ranges of outcomes, and sorting players into buckets based on similarity is one way to do that. It helps determine true consistency and volatility on the individual level, which is extremely valuable information.

But we also need to take a broader view of our lineups, determining how each piece of the puzzle fits together. I'm a big believer that intelligent lineup construction is sensationally valuable to daily fantasy players; I'd go as far as to say I think you can be a +EV daily fantasy player with some very basic risk evaluation coupled with shrewd lineup construction.

In most instances, one player's production doesn't affect that of another in your lineup. But when those players are in the same game, their performances are entangled. When the opponent of your quarterback runs the ball on 70 percent of their plays, the game gets shortened and it has a major impact on overall production. When your running back's wide receivers are studs in the red zone and facing small cornerbacks, it can cut into the back's touchdown probability in a massive way. The point is there are all sorts of ways in which teammates and opponents have correlated fantasy production. Leveraging those relationships in an intelligent manner is perhaps the most overlooked way of giving yourself proper exposure to a high ceiling.

The most notorious teammate relationship in daily fantasy football is that of a quarterback and one of his wide receivers. Pairing the two together is referred to as 'stacking' or 'handcuffing.' The idea is to increase your lineup's upside through correlations; when your wide receiver scores a touchdown, for example, you'll receive 10 points for that score—six from him and four from the quarterback. There's more risk with such a strategy—a poor day from your quarterback likely means the same for his wide receivers—but when it makes sense to take on risk to maximize upside (as in a tournament), stacking is almost a prerequisite for success.

To give an idea of the strength of this relationship, here's a look at the relationship between quarterback and wide receiver scoring on DraftKings...

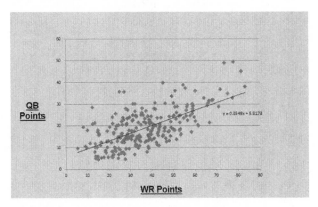

When a quarterback scores 20 points, the expectation for wide receivers is somewhere around 40 combined points.

When the passer hits 30 fantasy points, wide receiver scoring jumps to just under 70 points; that's a massive increase and displays how much upside there is in pairing your quarterback with at least one of his pass-catchers.

I also researched the probability of a quarterback and one of his receivers having a big day together, which is really what we want to know most.

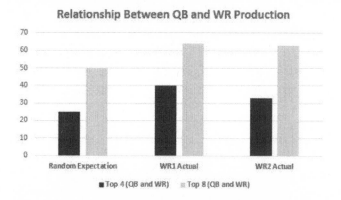

If performances were completely independent of one another, we'd expect a quarterback and wide receiver to have one of their top-four games coincide just 25 percent of the time and one of their top-eight games overlap 50 percent of the time. In reality, those numbers are 40 percent and 63 percent, respectively, for WR1s, i.e. there's clearly a greater probability of reaching a high ceiling when pairing a quarterback with his receivers.

But there's also more risk.

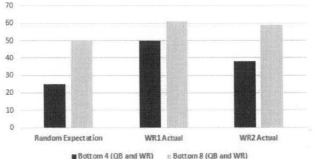

If production wasn't correlated, we'd again expect a quarterback and wide receiver to have a 25 percent overlap on bottom-four games and a 50 percent overlap on bottom-eight games. Those numbers are actually 50 percent and 61 percent, respectively.

Actually, I think this is perhaps evidence to generally forgo pairing a quarterback and WR1 in cash games; the correlation increases upside, but there's also a lot more risk (and actually I think there's a greater amount of risk than upside); when a quarterback tanks, his wide receivers have almost no chance of having a big game, whereas when the quarterback excels, certain wide receivers could still have underwhelming performances. Stacking is still a very viable strategy in GPPs— even if the risk outweighs the upside—but it's probably smart in cash games only with a very reliable tandem (such as Tom Brady and Julian Edelman, for example).

A wide receiver's production is correlated with that of his quarterback in a very obvious way, but other in-game relationships might not be so obvious. RotoViz recently published some amazing analysis showing the strength of correlation between players at every position in a game.

Correlational r-values range from -1 to 1, with the more extreme numbers representing the strongest correlations. A correlation of -0.8 represents a very strong inverse relationship (as one variable increases, the other decreases), a correlational strength of 0 means no relationship, and an r-value of 0.8 means a very strong positive relationship (as one increases, so does the other).

Using that research, here's a look at the strongest correlations in football.

K and Opposing D (-0.50)

This is a pretty obvious one—kicker scoring hurts your defense—but it's somewhat surprising this is the strongest correlation in fantasy football.

QB and Opposing D (-0.46)

Again, this should be fairly obvious. Don't start your quarterback (or any player at any position) against your defense.

K and Opposing K (-0.41)

This correlation is absolutely useless since you can't start two kickers in fantasy football. If you're in a season-long league in which you can, you absolutely need to reevaluate where your life has gone.

WR2 and QB on Same Team (0.39)

More so than any other pass-catchers, a WR2's production is most strongly connected with that of his quarterback. That doesn't mean the two have more upside than a QB/WR1 pairing—they don't—but just that a No. 2 wide receiver typically has his biggest games when his quarterback does, too, whereas a WR1's production comes just slightly more independently.

I also think this is one (small) piece of evidence that pairing your quarterback with his two top wide receivers has some value in tournaments. There's been a lot of discussion about this topic and if it actually cuts into upside, but there's a lot of meat left on the bone when you're talking about high-scoring games.

If you do plan to start a quarterback with two of his receivers, consider what types of receivers they are and which stats they rely on. I loved to start Tom Brady with both Julian Edelman and Rob Gronkowski (obviously not a wide receiver, but same effect) because Edelman scores fantasy points primarily via catching the ball a lot and Gronk relies more on touchdowns. The two don't cannibalize one another in the same way as, say, Mike Evans and Vincent Jackson.

WR3 and QB on Same Team (0.35)

A quarterback's production is pretty strongly linked to that of his No. 3 wide receiver. This correlation isn't surprising; if a No. 3 wide receiver goes off, chances are his quarterback had a monster day. There really isn't a time when it's appropriate to start a WR3, however, given the likely lack of targets.

QB and K on Same Team (0.35)

Kicker production is strongly tied to quarterback scoring. I don't think you're cutting into your upside too much by starting a kicker with a quarterback on the same team.

K and D on Same Team (0.35)

Kickers and defenses are also linked. I'm not entirely sure why this correlation is so strong.

WR1 and QB on Same Team (0.34)

Of a team's top three receivers, it's actually the WR1 with the weakest correlation to quarterback production. However, the strengths are all about the same. My guess is WR1 production is most independent of the quarterback because he sees the most targets, regardless of how the offense is moving the ball. A struggling quarterback will probably force the ball to his top wide receiver more than the other pass-catchers.

RB and Opposing RB (-0.31)

There's a strong negative correlation in fantasy production for opposing running backs. Even with pass-catching backs, I don't think it ever makes much sense to play two running backs in the same game.

Other than these correlations, there are a few other interesting relationships to note. One is that a running back's production is slightly negatively correlated with pass-catchers on his team. This is probably a true cannibalizing effect; every catch or touchdown for a wide receiver or tight end is a lack of points for the running back.

There's also no real correlation for two quarterbacks in the same game. There's a popular narrative that games can turn into shootouts and both quarterbacks can go off. I think that might be the case in certain instances—namely when the game is projected to be a tight, high-scoring battle—but overall, opposing quarterback production isn't linked.

Finally, I want to mention there's one other relationship you can take advantage of that basically provides upside for "free" with no additional risk: pairing a wide receiver or running back who returns kickoffs/punts with his D/ST. If you plan to use a wide receiver who returns punts, for example, as well as that team's defense and special teams, it makes sense to pair those two together whenever you can; if the player has a return touchdown, you get double the points—six from him and six from you D/ST. Although not particularly common, it's an easy way to increase upside without taking on risk.

The Bankroll of a Contrarian Player

There is no one-size-fits-all bankroll management plan. It seems to be widely accepted that you can put up to 10 percent of your bankroll into play each day, but such a plan of attack for an antifragile contrarian GPP player would be deadly.

If you have a normal distribution of tournament finishes and a 20 percent long-term ROI, you still have somewhere around a 16 percent chance of being down after a sample of 1,000 GPPs. You read that correctly. If you are a big long-term winner and play one tournament lineup per week, you have somewhere around a one-in-six chance of still being down after 62.5 seasons of NFL action.

We can get around this by playing slightly less optimal lineups, which will decrease long-term ROI but improve the probability of being profitable after X number of leagues. Either way, my point is there's a lot of variance in daily fantasy sports, especially one as infrequent as football. No matter how good you are, you're going to lose some weeks. You're even going to lose some months. You might even be the best player in the world and, by chance alone, be down after an entire season.

Now consider what it means to be a contrarian GPP player. We're (at times) purposely using players we know are not elite values—players who aren't maximizing our probability of cashing—in order to maximize the payoff when those players do hit. I do believe this style of play enhances the chances of winning a league, but it does so at the expense of a high cash rate. Our mentality is "If you aren't first, you're last," which might as well be "We're going to lose more than other players in exchange for occasional huge jumps in our bankroll."

These bankroll swings can be difficult to tolerate, especially if you aren't practicing proper bankroll management. You're inevitably going to go through cold stretches, and you need to be prepared to handle them. There's so much variance in GPPs—and even more so as a contrarian player—that you can't realistically place 10 percent of your bankroll into tournaments each week and think you have zero risk of ruin. That's fine if you understand the risks and want to take the chance, but realize you're significantly increasing your downside at that point.

I personally place around two to three percent of my bankroll into GPPs. I will occasionally go slightly higher in the event of overlay or when I otherwise believe I have a larger-than-normal edge (such as with important late-breaking news to which I've adjusted). But normally, that's all I'm risking.

Before Moving On

I hope I've been able to outline the foundation of my daily fantasy sports philosophy. In a nutshell, I think it's more challenging to predict performance than most. Site pricing and daily fantasy player selection tends to underestimate the amount of randomness inherent to sports outcomes, which I believe creates an inefficiency in the GPP market. Ownership rates on the chalk are too high—meaning you're getting poor odds to start those players—while certain against-the-grain selections lead to payoffs that exceed the risks. If you can get even money on an event that will happen 40 percent of the time or 10-to-1 odds on an event that will happen 15 percent of the time, you will go broke if you consistently choose the former and get rich if you steadily select the latter.

Of course, much of this discussion has been somewhat theoretical up until now. I embrace the role of philosophy and abstract thinking in DFS—especially in tournament play—but our decisions need to be governed by the numbers.

So that's what the rest of this book is dedicated toward—the data and stats you need to make superior decisions.

"The 50-50-90 rule: Anytime you have a 50-50 chance of getting something right, there's a 90% probability you'll get it wrong."

    Andy Rooney

III. Into the Lab: Testing Daily Fantasy Football Strategies

"Science is a way of life. Science is a perspective. Science is the process that takes us from confusion to understanding in a manner that's precise, predictive and reliable - a transformation, for those lucky enough to experience it, that is empowering and emotional."

Brian Greene

I met Peter Jennings (CSURAM88) in 2012. When I say we "met," I really mean we became online friends (only the best type of friend you can have these days, but it's whatever). But soon after that time, we realized we wanted to work together on a project in the daily fantasy space. He's been involved with some of my past books, but we never really were able to go all-in.

The problem was development. It's difficult as hell to find quality developers, and even more so to find someone who can do both front and back end development, understands how to build models, and understands sports/DFS.

Well, we finally found them in the beginning of 2015, and the result is Fantasy Labs. We teamed up with a group from Sports Insights—a popular sportsbetting site—so we not only got some of the best developers I've ever seen, but also access to a huge database of sports data.

We have all kinds of important Vegas information (line movements, live public betting data, and so on), as well as a wealth of other advanced analytics. More important, we have historical salary and performance data from the major DFS sites. With that, we're able to mix and match all these numbers to find specific trends and determine what truly leads to DFS value (not just what predicts quality play, but what predicts production minus cost).

For example, we know pass-catching ability is a plus for running backs in terms of fantasy. All else equal, we clearly want running backs who can contribute as receivers. But that doesn't mean it automatically leads to value in daily fantasy; if DraftKings has historically overvalued pass-catching ability in their pricing algorithm, we might see that pass-catching backs are actually overpriced as a whole.

With all this data, we were able to create a number of proprietary stats for DFS players. The most important of these is Plus/Minus. Simply put, a player's Plus/Minus is his actual points minus his expected points. So if Le'Veon Bell scored 150 points over the past 10 games and his expectation was 120 points, he would have a Plus/Minus of 30 total points, or +3.0 points per game.

Cool. So how do we know what to "expect" from each player? We know based on our database of historical salaries and fantasy performances on each daily fantasy site. Instead of using a fragile $/point system (or, even worse, sorting players into completely arbitrary tiers), we use actual performance data to help calculate exactly what to expect out of a player based on his cost. So if Bell costs $9,000 on DraftKings, we know he should produce X points, on average.

Using Plus/Minus, we can calculate all kinds of really cool stats and identify league-winning trends. Here are a few:

Consistency

Also known as 'X1,' our Consistency figures show the percentage of games in which a player has reached his salary-based expectation. Instead of assessing players in an arbitrary and artificial way, we look at how production on each site has historically been connected to pricing to determine a more natural expected point total. All players are placed on an even playing field; it is just as easy for a $5,000 player to reach X consistency as it is for a $3,000 player, for example.

Breakout/Upside

Also known as 'X2,' our Breakout/Upside figures show the percentage of games in which a player has reached *twice* his salary-based expectation.

Dud

Our Dud stat calculates the percentage of games in which a player has scored fewer than *half* his salary-based expectation.

Trends/Pro Trends

We also have a product called Trends that lets users leverage our massive database of historical salaries and fantasy performances to determine in which situations players traditionally offer value. You can create your own trends or utilize our DFS-pro-created 'Pro Trends,' which already show up in our other products.

Here's an example of a simple trend I created looking at the topic of pass-catching running backs. We have dozens of different filters you can set, so I just looked at the historic Plus/Minus on DraftKings for running backs who entered a game with at least 3.0 receptions per game over the past 12 months. Here's how those players performed last season...

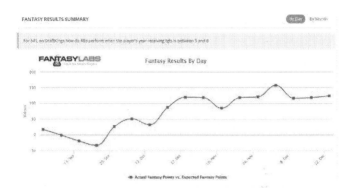

FANTASY RESULTS SUMMARY

For NFL on DraftKings how do RBs perform when the player's year receiving tgts is between 3 and 8

FANTASYLABS — Fantasy Results By Day

● Actual Fantasy Points vs. Expected Fantasy Points

Since Plus/Minus is based off of scoring expectations, an average score is zero. Anything negative means cost exceeded production (a lack of value) and anything positive means production exceeded cost (a good value).

Overall, running backs with at least 3.0 receptions per game over the past 12 months have a Plus/Minus of 0.28 points per game, i.e. they've scored 0.28 points per game more than what we'd expect based on their DraftKings salaries alone (based on the cost of each player, we would expect them to score 10.95 points per game, and they actually scored 11.23).

The Trends tool is so sick because you can find out what is and is not priced into DFS salaries literally in a matter of seconds. You can save your trends, identify past and current matches, and so on. It's a truly revolutionary product because you no longer need to guess about what leads to daily fantasy value; you can test everything immediately and figure out which factors DFS sites are accounting for and which ones they're missing (or not weighing heavily enough).

Player Models

With all this data, we're able to do some really cool stuff to ultimately help daily fantasy players build lineups. The most useful tool we have is called Player Models, which provides users the ability to very quickly create models, rank players (in an accurate way), backtest the model to see how well it would have performed in the past, and optimize lineups based off of any model created.

Here's a screenshot of our MLB Player Models...

The first part of this that's really cool is being able to see all the relevant data you need in one place. Peter and I have worked hard to make sure we display the stats and factors DFS players want to see. Instead of having five or 10 tabs open with all the information you need to build lineups, you can now visit just one site.

Second, you can very quickly build your own player models using the sliders on the left side of the screen. You tell us how much you want to weigh each stat or how important you think it is in predicting success at each position. We then rate each player by weighing those stats/factors in accordance with how you set them.

The most important part of all this is that each time you click 'Update,' we backtest the model. Basically, you can create a profitable DFS model in a matter of minutes (or use one of ours) because we're showing you what actually works. It's awesome.

As an example, you might want to weigh a player's weekly ceiling and his overall upside heavily if you're creating a tournament lineup. You can do that, and then we'll show you how the top players in that model performed in the past (in terms of Plus/Minus, Upside, Consistency, and so on).

Anyway, I won't get into too much detail here because you can check it out for yourself, but I did want to set the stage for a lot of the analysis in this chapter, most of which uses our proprietary stats and was generated using the Trends tool at Fantasy Labs.

The Bargain Rating

One of my favorite stats we created at Fantasy Labs is called "Bargain Rating," which is in its simplest form a measure of how cheap a player is on DraftKings or FanDuel versus the other site. We look at historic pricing at each position on each site, then calculate a player's percentile rank in terms of the difference.

For example, let's say the average quarterback costs $8000 on DraftKings and $7000 on FanDuel. If we were considering a quarterback with those exact price tags on the respective sites in a given week, his Bargain Rating would be 50—not a bargain more so on one site than the other. However, if he cost $7000 on both sites, he'd have a higher Bargain Rating on DraftKings (maybe 70 or so) and a lower Bargain Rating on FanDuel (maybe about 30).

The idea behind the Bargain Rating is two-fold. First and foremost, it's a way to find value. Site pricing reflects a site's best guess at how a player will perform in a given week. If FanDuel has Aaron Rodgers as the most expensive quarterback and DraftKings has him at No. 4, chances are he's somewhere between those two in terms of his weekly projection. Either way, he'd be likely overpriced on FanDuel and underpriced on DraftKings—or at the very least, more likely to be underpriced on the latter site.

The other way that the Bargain Rating is useful is simply to see where players are priced the cheapest. Instead of spending all kinds of time figuring that out, we have a simple number reflecting the percentile rank of the sites' salary difference. If a player is wildly cheaper on DraftKings than FanDuel and has a 99 Bargain Rating, that's a great sign he's underpriced. Basically, it's an easy and effective way to shop for the best prices.

So I could talk all day about why buying guys at the cheapest possible price is a profitable strategy, or I could just use the Fantasy Labs Trends tool to show you. Using the tool's various stats and filters, I looked solely at last season's quarterbacks on DraftKings who had a Bargain Rating of at least 90, i.e. the difference between their salary on DraftKings and FanDuel ranked in the 90th percentile or better historically.

There's a clear upward trend here, with these quarterbacks leading to a positive Plus/Minus (i.e. good value) in 56.3 percent of the weeks studied. And typically, they outperformed salary-based expectations by a whole lot when they did it.

QBs With 90 Bargain Rating NFL-QB-DRAFTKINGS

Count 🛈	Avg Expected Pts 🛈	Avg Actual Pts 🛈	Points +/- 🛈
60	14.63	18.00	3.36

There were 60 quarterbacks with a Bargain Rating of 90 or
better last year, and based on their salaries, they averaged
14.63 expected points. If they were priced perfectly, we'd see
their actual points also at 14.63. But at 18.00 points per
game, the quarterbacks had a Plus/Minus of +3.36, which is
massive—23 percent more points than we'd expect based on
their cost. By looking at nothing more than the inefficiencies
in quarterback salaries between DraftKings and FanDuel, you
could have added 3.36 expected points last season, basically
for nothing.

And it isn't just quarterbacks. I charted the Plus/Minus for the
main four positions, sorting their performances into buckets
based on their Bargain Ratings: 0-20, 21-40, 41-60, 61-80, 81-
100, 90+, and 95+.

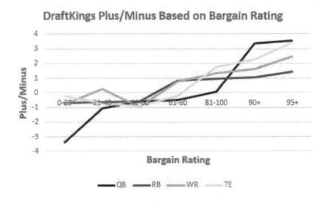

Holy crap. There's a lot going on here, but the most obvious
trend is that every position benefits massively from a high
Bargain Rating. It's so strong that I think you could make an
argument that you could potentially be a profitable player by

doing nothing except optimizing a lineup around a site's cheapest players. By paying as little as possible, you're leaving as much possible meat on the bone as possible for players to generate value.

Here's another look at the data, this time as a heatmap...

	Bargain Rating						
	0-20	21-40	41-60	61-80	81-100	90+	95+
QB	-3.38	-1.07	-0.61	-0.48	0.07	3.36	3.54
RB	-0.71	-0.66	-0.59	0.81	0.94	1.06	1.43
WR	-0.78	0.26	-0.96	0.76	1.33	1.62	2.48
TE	-0.24	-0.75	-0.92	-0.2	1.76	2.29	3.42

Some thoughts...

1. This is basically an analysis of how much it pays to be price-sensitive at each position. If price didn't matter much—if there was enough randomness in the sport that value wasn't that important—these lines wouldn't be so steep. The larger the difference in value based on Bargain Rating, the more the cost matters and the more a player's salary should dictate your decision to roster him or not.

2. The largest discrepancy is at quarterback, by far. That makes sense when you consider that quarterback play is the most predictable of any position, thus making price a larger predictor of value. If you look at players who had a Bargain Rating of 0 to 20 on DraftKings (players who were poor values as compared to their price on FanDuel), three of the four positions had a Plus/Minus no worse than -0.78. Meanwhile, quarterback was at -3.38, which is pretty crazy.

3. If you did nothing but play quarterbacks with a Bargain Rating of 95 or higher, you could be expected to score an average of 6.92 DraftKings points more than if you played solely those with a Bargain Rating from 0 to 20. That's nearly seven points just from looking at pricing.

4. Running back was on the other end of the spectrum with a difference of just 2.14 points. That's a bit surprising. It could be that DraftKings prices their running backs more accurately, although I do think there's some merit to the idea that you don't need to be as price-sensitive at the position as at some others. The reason is there are often very clear must-play guys at times—backup running backs who get thrust into the starting lineup come to mind—such that it doesn't matter if they're a bit more expensive on one site than the other; they're still sensational values. A backup who is going to see a heavy workload is going to be very likely to provide value regardless of whether he costs $3,000 or $4,500.

5. It's pretty interesting that no position in the 41-60 range has a positive Plus/Minus. I'd imagine that's evidence of the most underpriced players—those with the highest Bargain Rating—providing a disproportional amount of the value in daily fantasy football. The jump in Plus/Minus that we see from even 90+ to 95+ lends more credence to that idea.

6. I want to mention that Bargain Rating is powerful, but it isn't going to capture every underpriced player. It's very possible that both DraftKings and FanDuel underrate a player's upside, in which case he might have a 50 Bargain Rating yet still be underpriced. And the opposite is true for overpriced players, too. Nonetheless, it's still an extremely valuable stat for both identifying value and quickly shopping for prices. Even if you don't use Bargain Rating as a predictive tool—which it appears to be—it can still have value just for finding where players are the cheapest, which gives you the largest buffer when it comes to protecting yourself from measurement errors.

Bargain Shopping in DFS

My mom calls me like once a week to tell me about all the amazing deals she recently found. "I went to the farmer's market and got these old wooden chairs that I'm going to restore. Only $50 for four of them. I'm going to sand them down, fix some of the wood, and paint them and they'll look amazing." She fucking loves deals. Every aging mom does. My mom doesn't read my books so I can label her as 'aging.' But it's like the moment a kid leaves home, his or her mom instantly becomes the biggest bargain hunter you've ever seen in your life.

Then every Christmas I go home and I open up a present (I'm not yet 30 so waking up at 6am to open gifts at my mother's house on X-Mas morning is still acceptable, IMO) and she immediately brags about the price. I swear she's just buying us more and more stuff so she can tell everyone how much it cost.

Begins to open gift

"It's a sweater! $15 at Marshall's—on sale from $100. It was originally $100. Can you believe that? Isn't it great? Fif-teen-fucking dollars Jonathan! Down from $100! Originally cost $100, now $15!"

My mom is a drug addict and her drug of choice is #greatdeals.

I'm not nearly as price-sensitive as her. As has been well-documented on Twitter, I order delivery food almost every day. People say it costs so much more than getting groceries. Does it though? When I get groceries, I need to go to the supermarket and pay X dollars, bring everything back and put it away, cook when I want something to eat, and do the dishes (I use paper and plastic like a boss but when I run out I do have to make my way into the fine china). None of it tastes as good as delivery, the food spoils, and there are a million things wrong with it...namely that I need to leave my house, which is frightening to even think about. My process for ordering food is click button, wait, eat food. Much simpler and honestly I think ultimately *less* expensive given the reduced opportunity cost.

I don't go out of my way to get #greatdeals on old-ass wooden chairs at flea markets is all I'm saying.

However, there are times when I transform into the daily fantasy sports version of my mom, shopping for deals and finding the best possible goods at the cheapest possible prices. When all else is equal, I actually want to be as price-sensitive as possible at all times. With every pick I make, I ask "How can I replicate this expected production at a cheaper price?" If I can do it, I will do it.

Cheaper is (usually) better in DFS because 1) it leaves more room for error (and there will always be assessment errors) and 2) it allows for more flexibility. Unlike in real-life bargain hunting, there's no opportunity cost associated with DFS bargain hunting. Less money spent here means more money there without any additional time requirement. It's not like I need to do a complex calculation to figure out the running back who costs $5,000 and is projected at 15 points is better than the one who costs $6,000 and is projected to score the same.

This is obviously the concept behind the Bargain Rating at Fantasy Labs—pay as little as possible when you can. Even if you play on only one site, though, your goal is still to find X production and pay as little as possible for it. Anticipated Production − Cost = Value.

There are a ton of ways to do that, one of which that I believe is underrated is to study site pricing changes.

Site Pricing and Randomness

The reason I care about pricing changes so much is related to my views on randomness. The degree to which we need to be price-sensitive is directly related to how much randomness is inherent to a sport. If we could perfectly predict outcomes, there wouldn't be any reason to care about site pricing changes; we'd just want to maximize anticipated production minus cost, regardless of pricing.

However, we don't always know anticipated production. We can estimate it—we can come close, perhaps—but there's still a large element of luck involved with sports outcomes. However, people often treat events as though they're always a reflection of reality.

When a player appears to be slumping, his salary will sometimes decline. If that slump is an illusion, he's going to offer value. But—and here's the most important point—even if that slump is real, he could still offer value if the price drops too much.

Basically, what I think happens is that we see Player X turn in three straight poor games, and his price drops as though he's 100 percent in a slump. And maybe he is. But maybe the chances he's truly slumping—and by that, I mean he hasn't just been unlucky—are just a coin flip. Then we're getting great odds to take a chance on a player whose past poor production might have been random and not predictive of any sort of poor future performance.

The key is that overreaction, both by DFS sites and the general public. When a player is "cold"—as in he's had a few bad games in a row, regardless of the cause (or if there's a cause)—his price might drop as though we know exactly what is going on. But we don't; we need to factor in the uncertainty we should have regarding game outcomes. When we do that, the anticipated production often jumps such that players whose salary has dropped tend to offer value, or at least a probability of performing at a high level that isn't reflected in their cost. Sites overcompensate with pricing.

So do DFS players. When a player is cold, his ownership in both cash games and tournaments decreases. When he's hot, his ownership increases. This is true in every single sport. The crowd is not very price-sensitive and instead overemphasizes recent results. It's one of the largest DFS inefficiencies to exploit.

That's especially true in football because, again, we have to wait a week between games—seven long days that allow the media to construct narratives that people buy into. *Of course* that stud running back with 70 total yards in the first two weeks of the season is done and should be benched; it couldn't be that two fluky unfavorable game scripts cut into his production. *Of course* the rookie wide receiver with two touchdowns last week is about to break out; it couldn't be that he was lucky to score twice when he saw only three targets.

Basically, we're not only getting value by jumping on players whose salaries have declined (or avoiding landmines by fading hot players—Eric Decker, amirite?—whose salaries have recently risen), but we're also creating a natural contrarian strategy without forgoing value (or getting away from the crowd on overhyped players).

It's a win-win...just pick players who have played like total garbage lately and watch the money roll in! No, seriously, that's like 90% of my DFS strategy.

The Data on Pricing Fluctuations

Numbers.

Salary Change (Season)	QB	RB	WR	TE
Dropped >2000	1.11	0.87	2.30	N/A
Dropped 1001-2000	1.77	0.44	1.98	2.78
Dropped 0-1000	0.07	-0.24	0.02	0.01
Increased 0-1000	-0.89	-0.30	-0.44	-0.54
Increased 1001-2000	-0.81	0.98	-2.52	-0.92
Increased >2000	-4.76	0.11	-0.34	-5.58

This is a look at the Plus/Minus of players in games when their salary has changed X dollars from the start of the season. For example, quarterbacks in games in which their salary is over $2000 lower than Week 1 have performed 1.11 DraftKings points above salary-based expectation. There's a very clear relationship here for every position; salary decreases are good, salary increases are bad. That's a general rule-of-thumb, of course, but one that leads to a shitload of value.

Remember, this is all about site pricing. Players whose salaries drop generally aren't playing well of late. Some of that might be due to repeatable factors, but much of it is likely randomness. If it's more of the latter than the former but DraftKings is acting as if it's mostly the former, you get overcompensation which can lead to value on "cold" players and a lack of value on "hot" ones.

After looking at these numbers on the seasonal level, I thought it might be more appropriate (and perhaps more telling to examine monthly salary changes). Here's a look at the change in Plus/Minus based on salary movement over a running 30-day period.

Salary Change (Month)	QB	RB	WR	TE
Dropped >1500	4.20	3.24	2.26	0.61
Dropped 501-1500	1.41	1.18	1.67	1.72
Dropped 0-500	-0.26	-0.37	-0.18	-0.08
Increased 0-500	-0.70	-0.35	-0.49	-0.34
Increased 501-1500	-0.96	-0.51	-1.02	-1.42
Increased >1500	-1.36	0.33	-0.33	-1.77

These results are even more extreme than on the seasonal level, which I think makes sense. Monthly salary changes are almost always a reaction to recent play and/or current matchup strength. If DraftKings is overreacting to those factors, we'll get value on players whose salaries decline. The numbers on players whose prices have dropped even $500 are substantial.

Here's an example to show just how extreme these results are. If you were to blindly select an entire lineup of salary-droppers and match it up against one of exclusively salary-risers—and we'll define each as a change in salary of between $501 and $1500, either up or down—the lineup of salary-droppers would outscore the salary-risers by an average of 19.65 points on DraftKings (not including a defense), assuming you use a wide receiver in the flex. Nineteen-point-six-five-gosh-darn points!

To me, this is extreme evidence that daily fantasy pricing is way, way more of a reflection of recent play than it should be, failing to properly account for variance. I truly believe salary changes are a very powerful way to acquire value, especially in a sport like daily fantasy football in which there are very few games and everyone tends to overreact to small sample sizes of results.

We track salary changes on the season and monthly levels at Fantasy Labs. You can also incorporate those factors into any model you create to automatically account for the power of salary movement.

Before moving on, I think it's worth mentioning that I believe this method of analysis has value not only in cash games—in which Plus/Minus is extremely relevant—but also in tournaments. Especially in a sport like football, the public loves to play favorites. When a guy breaks out and his price jumps, they're generally all over him. More so than in any sport, there isn't a whole lot of price-sensitivity in daily fantasy football.

Because of that, the value of jumping on salary-droppers is two-fold; you get the extra value that stems from the price reduction, but you often times can also benefit from reduced GPP ownership. We're always trying to balance value and ownership in tournaments, so when we can get both at a premium level, we're going to make money.

Does Streaky Play Exist?
Does streaky play exist? Yes.

Okay, that settles that. You're just going to have to take my word for it.

That's actually sort of how the majority of DFS and sports content is written. Pose question, offer opinion, move on.

I do think it seems natural that some form of streaky play exists. While I attribute an extremely large degree of randomness to sports results—more so than most stat nerds I know—I also think it would be naïve to say everything is random and there's no such thing as momentum (in any sense of the word), or that players don't at all go through hot and cold streaks. Certainly there are times when players are performing with more or less confidence than others, or when a running back's offensive line is just dominating and giving him huge holes, or when a quarterback can't miss a receiver, or whatever.

But the streaky play argument—the idea that players go through ups and downs that are more than just random fluctuations—is very much like the topic of injury proneness or batter vs pitcher data in baseball; there's a difference between a phenomenon existing and us being able to use that information to make accurate forecasts.

Let's take injury proneness, for example. Are some football players more likely to get hurt or more likely to require a bunch of time to heal than others? Yeah, probably. It would be foolish to think Player X's body type and genetics wouldn't make his injury exposure and healing ability different than that from Player Y.

However, injuries are such a low-frequency event that it's really difficult to separate them from randomness. Maybe the running back who tore his ACL is injury-prone, or maybe he just got unlucky. Only when we have a pretty massive history of injuries can we label someone as truly injury-prone (it's also the case that injury proneness isn't binary; there's likely a range of injury proneness, and determining where someone falls on that range is challenging given that guys aren't getting injured every day).

Same thing with BvP data. Sure, we'd expect certain hitters to truly crush certain pitchers and struggle versus others, but BvP has proven to lack predictive ability because the sample sizes are just way too small. When a batter is 5-for-10 off of a pitcher, we really have no idea if he will continue to hit him well or if he just got lucky in the past.

For the most part, I think we see something similar with perceived streaky play. Of course players go through hot and cold streaks—no one is denying that—but the real question is whether or not we can use past streaky play to predict future production. If not, then the pragmatic value of streaky play—whether it "exists" or not—is nil.

I want to go a step further. I want to not only know what sort of predictive ability streaky play might have, but also how well it can predict future DFS value. That is, does DraftKings account for any potential value streaky play might offer when they price players?

Before diving in, I want to mention this data is of course similar (but not exactly comparable) to the numbers on salary movement. Recent performance is of course a large factor in site pricing—one I believe is too large of a factor—but it isn't all that matters. There's a lot of overlap between salary movement and streaky play, but it isn't a perfect correlation. There are times when a struggling player might still move up in price because of a really juicy matchup, or due to an injury, or whatever.

We know players whose price drops tend to offer value and we know many players whose salary declines are those who appear to be struggling, but that doesn't mean all struggling players see their salary plummet or that all "cold" players offer value. So keep that in mind as we view these results; we don't just want to jump on slumping players for the hell of it; it only has value following a reduction in price (and often a substantial one).

Anyway, I used the Trends tool at Fantasy Labs to research historic value offered by players coming off of one, two, or three consecutive games in which they exceeded their salary-based expectation. Based on historic scoring, for example, we know quarterbacks who cost $8,000 needed to score just over 21 fantasy points to reach value—a bit less than 3x their salary. The data I collected shows the value (Plus/Minus) offered by players in the midst of what we'd consider a "hot streak" of sorts, so we can determine if jumping on those hot streaks offers value.

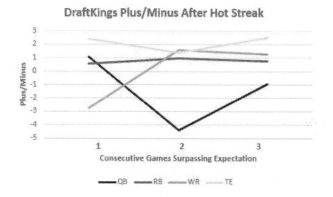

This is a whole lot of nothing. There really aren't any trends here. Quarterbacks who have exceeded their expected points in two/three straight games have performed well below what we'd expect in the subsequent contest, although the sample is admittedly small at just a few dozen passers.

The Plus/Minus numbers are positive for 10 of the 12 data points, but barely. The overall Plus/Minus is +0.36 points, but the results don't inspire much confidence. If hot streaks were truly predictive, for example, we might expect players to perform better coming off of three consecutive above-average games as compared to two, and better off of two as compared to one, etc...but we don't.

I'm sure there's some sort of correlation between hot streaks and future production, but it's probably a weak one. Further, it appears to be at least mostly priced into DraftKings salaries. I don't think there's an advantage to be had here.

But now let's examine "cold" players...

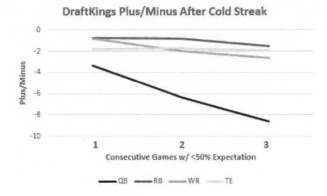

Again, 12 data points, and every single one is below zero. Following just a single game of poor play, players at all four skill positions turn in a negative Plus/Minus. It gets worse after two poor games, and even worse after three.

This is really interesting because it suggests cold streaks are "real" and hot streaks aren't (or at least they don't offer DraftKings value). I have some thoughts here, but first let's compare the average Plus/Minus for "hot" and "cold" players at each position.

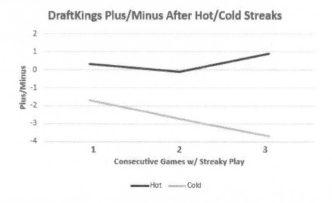

Again, there's perhaps a minor effect with players on hot streaks, but it isn't statistically significant. Also, the fact that it isn't a linear relationship is troublesome. My guess is that there's probably a weak correlation between recent quality performances and future production, but DraftKings mostly compensates for it in their pricing. I don't think it makes sense to go out of your way to ride hot streaks. Plus, don't forget the public is generally all over those players, so you also run into ownership issues in tournaments.

With cold streaks, however, there does indeed appear to be a relationship here. After two poor performance in a row, in particular, players are really underachieving relative to their salaries. Why?

I think there are more ways a cold streak can be "real" than a hot streak. Sure, lots of it is randomness, but players might also underachieve due to an injury or a change in workload. Both of those things can significantly alter expected production and are likely to affect performance moving forward, whereas hot streaks seem to be more randomness-driven and really challenging to use in a predictive manner.

So to recap…

1. Don't specifically target hot players, especially after a salary bump. That's doubly true in GPPs. Those players might or might not be "hot," but they're also likely to be overpriced and widely utilized by the public.

2. Do target players whose salaries have dropped (assuming there isn't a serious reason for concern about that pricing change, such as an injury or a major change in role).

3. Don't target cold players who haven't seen a major change in price. It isn't that cold players are "due" and inherently offer value, but rather that their reduced price becomes attractive. If you don't see that price reduction, there's no value to be had.

Wind Speed and Fantasy Value

They say don't sweat the small stuff, but I think one of the easiest ways to profit in daily fantasy is to do just that, focusing on the minor details that add up to a huge advantage in aggregate. This section is (eventually) going to be on wind speed, but I first want to post an excerpt from an old RotoAcademy lesson of mine that explains why I concentrate on the small stuff.

I write a lot of words on topics that might at times seem trivial. Someone on Twitter messaged me recently and said "Why do you focus on such minor shit? It's useless."

Obviously I disagree that what I do is useless, but I'd have to agree that I tend to harp on traits or events that, in certain contexts, can be deemed as "minor." But there's a method to my madness.

The reason that I take a "niche" approach to fantasy football is because I believe that the sum of those minor advantages—many of which can be acquired with a very small return on my time—will add up to something large.

Here's my attempt to explain why I think that's the case.

I've mentioned that daily fantasy football is a market. It's very much the same as the stock market. Every stock has value at a certain price (and every stock is also a poor value at a certain point); it's all about a comparison of future production and cost.

When we're trying to find actual value, we're really comparing how "inherent value" matches up with both site pricing and public perception; if the salary or public perception of a player's value is lower than his inherent value, he'll offer actual value. Since I tend to lean toward GPPs since I think they'll offer the greatest long-term ROI as daily fantasy evolves, I'm going to focus on value as a function of a player's projection relative to public opinion.

Uncovering inefficiencies in public perception is easier said than done. We know the general public is going to value common stats—like yards and touchdowns—as well as other obvious traits. Those things might be important in projecting a player, but they aren't going to help us obtain actual daily fantasy value because they're already priced into a player's ownership (and probably his salary, too).

Thus, to find usable value, our attention must naturally be skewed to those traits or stats that are unappreciated—often those considered "minor." I focus on the details not only because they're predictive, but because others aren't and it creates a potentially large advantage for me.

I have a ton of data showing weight is more important than speed for wide receivers. But let's assume it weren't. Let's assume for a second that size and speed mattered exactly the same for wide receivers. Which one is more useful?

Most would answer that they're equally useful; if they're equally predictive, they must have the same value to teams. That might be true in a vacuum, but the correct answer is that, in a market, the measurable with the most actual value would be the one that's least utilized by others.

In the real world, the public perception of speed is that it's more important than weight; teams fall in love with fast wide receivers and completely account for that speed during the actual NFL Draft, sometimes even overdoing it (see Tavon Austin).

Does speed matter for wide receivers? Yeah, of course; it matters for every position, some more than others. The idea here isn't only how predictive speed is for receivers or how much it matters on the field, but rather how fully teams are accounting for it in their actions. And because they really value straight-line speed, you generally can't find value on receivers by emphasizing it, even though it matters.

Another example is how teams grade running backs. Emphasizing quickness, many NFL teams are bullish on backs who time well in the short shuttle, even though it's a useless drill for predicting NFL success. While the 40-yard dash and broad jump are incredibly predictive of NFL success for running backs, the short shuttle has basically zero predictive ability.

But here's where things get a little weird; even though the short shuttle doesn't help identify quality running backs, you should still care about it. How is that possible? Public perception. Since teams value the short shuttle, they'll often draft players they deem as "quick" higher than those with elite straight-line speed. Since you know the short shuttle doesn't matter in terms of predicting great running backs but that it's still a component of cost, you should purposely seek out backs who dropped because of a lackluster short shuttle (but those who were above-average in the 40-yard dash or broad jump). There's massive value in going against the grain. That can mean seeking "underachievers" in areas that don't matter much but are still deemed important by the rest of the market, or by bypassing *"overachievers" in areas that the market values too much. No matter what, an understanding of how the market will react to certain stats/measurables/traits is a central component of finding value.*

In his book David and Goliath: Underdogs, Misfits, and the Art of Battling Giants, Malcolm Gladwell suggests that, for a variety of reasons, it's suitable to be a big fish in a small pond than vice versa. This idea is exactly why it's preferable to focus on small, "minor," underappreciated traits.

In effect, we're trying to increase our market share of exploitable advantages by decreasing the number of people with which we need to compete. Something can't be exploitable if it's overvalued by the public, so it follows that it's advantageous to focus on acquiring big pieces of smaller potential advantages—those of which people aren't aware or aren't valuing.

Ultimately, we're not looking for the most important traits in some philosophical sense, but just the ones that can lead to the biggest advantage over the field. That's calculated by subtracting public perception from inherent value (or its predictive ability). Thus, we get the big-fish-in-a-small-pond effect; by focusing on a bunch of "minor" traits that are highly exploitable, the aggregate advantage can be massive.

Finally, note that some traits can have negative value. If you recall, the short shuttle isn't predictive for running backs, but it's still priced into their cost to some degree. In that case, when we subtract the public perception of the short shuttle's importance (some positive figure) from its inherent value (zero or

*close to it), we necessarily get a negative number,
which informs us that it would be smart to target
running backs who have other predictors of success
but who struggle in the short shuttle.*

Okay, so that was 1,000+ words to justify why the hell I'm
talking about wind speed. In a nutshell, it isn't accounted for
by the market—whether "the market" is meant to represent
a daily fantasy site and their pricing or other DFS players
against whom you must compete.

DraftKings obviously can't account for anticipated wind speed
when they set their player salaries. Certainly wind speed isn't
naturally as important of a factor as, say, touchdown
probability, but if DraftKings perfectly prices touchdown
probability into their salaries, wind speed would offer more
usable value. They can't possibly account for wind speed,
which is why I love to examine it, along with similar flexible
factors: injuries, Vegas line movement, and so on.

Further, we know that Joe Schmoe doesn't give a shit about
how hard the wind is blowing in the Raiders-Broncos game,
so there's an advantage to be had over the field as well.

I've done some previous research on the effects of wind on
passing efficiency. Here are those results...

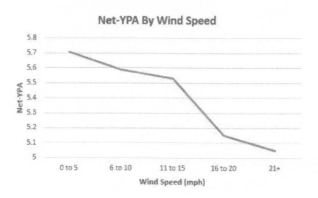

When wind is blowing around 15mph or faster, passing efficiency drops around 10 percent or so. That would turn a 300-yard performance into a 270-yard game. The actual numbers are even more extreme because coaches call fewer passing plays in windy games, which 1) directly hurts a quarterback's workload, obviously and 2) shortens the game so fewer plays are run overall, indirectly hurting all players' fantasy production.

Since we know wind speed can't possibly be a component of DraftKings' player pricing, we'd expect these numbers to extend to actual player value in terms of Plus/Minus. And they do.

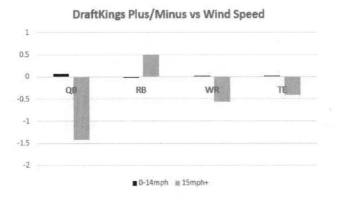

When winds are below 15mph, every position has basically an even Plus/Minus, meaning they're priced close to appropriately. But look at the Plus/Minus in windy games— down significantly for quarterbacks and pass-catchers, but up for running backs. That fits with the common sense explanation that wind hurts the passing game, but potentially helps running backs due to a slightly increased workload.

One question I had was how much pass-catching running backs are helped relative to others. Is it the case that teams run the ball more, or do quarterbacks just check it down more frequently when there are really strong winds?

The answer appears to be the former. Last season, running backs saw two or fewer targets in 77.2 percent of games with winds of at least 15mph, compared to only 73.8 percent of games with slower wind speeds. There was a greater occurrence of games with no more than one target, too. Strong winds can greatly limit passing efficiency, but they don't appear to have a major effect on running back targets.

Temperature and Fantasy Value

Like with heavy winds, cold temperatures can wreak havoc on a passing game.

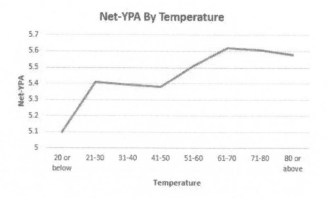

My hypothesis has been that very cold temperatures make it difficult to grip and throw a football. Whatever the case, cold temperatures don't result in a lighter passing load for quarterbacks like heavy winds. Thus, running backs don't benefit in the same manner.

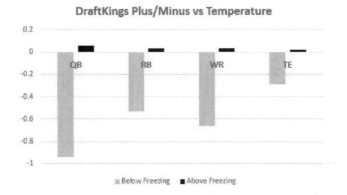

When the temperature has been above freezing—almost all games—all positions have seen a slightly positive Plus/Minus on DraftKings. It's basically negligible. When the temperature has been below freezing, though, players have lost a lot of value

Like wind speed, temperature is something for which DraftKings isn't really going to account when they price players early in the week. I don't think the temperature has as much potential impact on a game as really strong winds, but I do think you should be wary of ultra-cold games—the sub-zero battles at Lambeau and Solider Field late in the season—when it comes to seeking offensive upside.

One last thing…I have a confession: I have a hand fetish. Over the past year or two, I've spent way too much time researching the effects of hand size for football players, especially quarterbacks. I've found some really cool data that you can read about online (just search "Jonathan Bales Hand Monster" and it comes up…it really does) that shows how predictive hand size is of quarterback success.

Chip Kelly was the one who initially turned me on…to this idea. I was reading an old manifesto he created while coaching at Oregon in which he hypothesized that big hands allow a quarterback to control a football and throw it with accuracy. And he was very, very right.

Well, if quarterbacks as a whole struggle in cold weather because they perhaps have problems gripping the ball, we'd expect the majority of the struggles to come from small-handed passers. And overall, quarterbacks with below-average hand size (which is around 9.6 inches) have a larger change in statistics in below-freezing temperatures as compared to passers with above-average hand size. The change is about one percentage point in completion rate and an additional 0.3 interceptions per game.

Passing Efficiency

I clearly get a boner for obscure NFL stats. I can't even stand up in public after debating the value of hand size for quarterbacks.

What's so cool about our Plus/Minus data at Fantasy Labs is that, because we adjust everything based on daily fantasy site salaries, we can quickly determine not only which stats matter in terms of predicting usable value—which ones are priced into site salaries, and which aren't.

In a vacuum, a stat like Adjusted Yards Per Attempt is wildly more important than something like wind speed in predicting overall performance. It isn't even close. But it's a lot closer when you start talking about daily fantasy value. Adjusted Yards Per Attempt—a stat that considers yards, touchdowns, and picks (all components of fantasy scoring) is certainly priced into player salaries. It might not be perfect, but it isn't like there's no correlation between a quarterback's efficiency and his salary. The little shit isn't priced in—certain variables like weather can't even be a component of pricing even in theory, really—so that's why I emphasize it.

Here's a look at Adjusted YPA and DraftKings Plus/Minus...

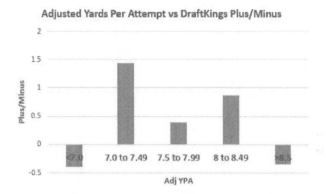

There's basically nothing here. Quarterbacks who have been below-average in Adjusted YPA in the 7.0 to 7.49 range have secured the most historic value on DraftKings. That could only be the case if the stat is priced into salaries.

So do we want quarterbacks who suck? Nah, call me crazy, but I still want good ones. But the point is you need to look past "How many yards has this guy thrown for?" and "How efficient has he been?" to "How much is this stat or angle priced into a player's salary and does anticipated production exceed the cost?"

Week-to-Week Consistency

One of my goals is to never have a real job. My favorite comedian Mitch Hedberg had a joke "I used to be a hot-tar roofer. Yeah, I remember that...day."

Well I had a job once working for a moving company. I was 17. It was a friend of my mom's and his company was struggling to find employees and I was supposed to work there for the entire summer. I worked for like six hours. If time flowed in reality as it did in my head, then I did indeed work the entire summer.

They called me at 3am the next morning to come in for another job. I said I was really sick. I wasn't sick. They called again the next morning and I said I had a baseball game later in the afternoon and didn't want to be tired. I didn't have a baseball game. So yeah, I used to be a mover. I remember that...day.

It was after those six hours of moving like three things with most of the other guys doing the work and me barely hanging on and just making faces of struggle and grunting a lot that I decided that working wasn't for me. I said I would never ever work for someone else ever again.

So far, I haven't. I'm almost 30 now and I still have never had a "real" job. I think a lot of people think that's really risky, but the riskiest thing you can do is not take chances, get paid a fraction of what you're worth as an employee, and have 100 percent of your income come from a single source. Seems pretty fragile to me.

Instead of trying to make money from a single source, I've tried to diversify as much as possible. I write, play DFS, sell stuff, run Fantasy Labs and RotoAcademy, author books, do some side coaching, refer people to play, etc. I think you could make an argument I'm too invested in one industry, which might be the case, although that's a calculated risk I've taken. Within DFS, though, I've tried to build the most stable income by generating revenue through as many avenues as I can. If my books stop selling, that would suck, but I'd be fine. If I can't make money playing anymore, that would also suck, but I would be fine. I try not to have more than 40 percent of my income stem from any single source, which I believe creates safety.

For a long time, I've had a hypothesis that a similar phenomenon is true in football; the players who generate their numbers in the most diverse manner should be the safest. And anecdotally, I've found that to be true. Quarterbacks who can run the ball and throw, running backs who catch a lot of passes, and wide receivers/tight ends who see a lot of short targets have been on my list of players to seek when I want week-to-week consistency (usually, but not always, in cash games).

Running Backs

I've been particularly interested in running backs because I think their production is more dependent on game flow than any other. Quarterback production tends to even out over the course of a game—winning teams usually get up by passing and then run late and losing teams tend to struggle passing early but make up for it with bulk attempts—but running back production doesn't flow in the same way. If a team gets down early, for example, there are certain backs who can continue to produce (Matt Forte) and those who are rendered basically useless (Alfred Morris).

I've completed some past research on running back consistency, but never through the scope of daily fantasy football (and especially never after accounting for salaries). I'm going to do that now.

If you recall, the Consistency Rating we created at Fantasy Labs is a measure of how often a player matches his expected points. Since our expected points are based on actual historic data, though, they place everyone on an even playing field. Unlike in other projection and rating systems, we don't overweight the value of cheap players. So you're just as likely to see a stud running back with a high Consistency Rating as a crap one.

So again, my theory has been that pass-catching backs have a lot more week-to-week consistency than running backs who don't catch a ton of passes; the latter group is dependent on a particular game script for production, and if things don't go their team's way early, they're shit out of luck.

Now, there are different ways to address this. One thing I like to do before anything is simply look at the top and bottom buckets in a particular statistical category and see what similarities there are. I realize there are more rigorous ways to analyze data, but I also want to take as efficient as an approach as possible. Sometimes, if you see very extreme results when analyzing two contrasting groups of players, it's a sign there's probably something there.

To scratch the surface, I charted the top 10 running backs from last year in terms of consistency, examining only backs with a minimum of 10 DraftKings points per game. Here they are.

		Consistency	Receptions/Game
1	Fred Jackson	71%	4.71
2	Ahmad Bradshaw	70%	3.80
3	Jeremy Hill	68%	1.69
4	DeMarco Murray	68%	3.56
5	Tre Mason	66%	1.33
6	Lamar Miller	62%	2.38
7	Ronnie Hillman	62%	2.63
8	Matt Asiata	60%	2.93
9	Matt Forte	56%	6.38
10	Eddie Lacy	56%	2.63
		Avg Rec/Game	3.25

Based on his week-to-week salaries, Fred Jackson was the most consistent back in the NFL last season, reaching his expectation 71 percent of the time. This isn't a list of solely mediocre backs, however; we also see Jeremy Hill, DeMarco Murray, Matt Forte, and Eddie Lacy.

Overall, this group averaged 3.25 receptions per game. Over the course of a 16-game season, that equates to 52 catches, which is a lot. Actually, that number would have tied for fifth among all running backs in the league last season. Considering we're looking at 10 running backs, that's pretty crazy. So this end of the extreme—the most consistent players—is made up almost exclusively of backs who double as receivers; only Hill and Mason had fewer than 2.35 receptions per game.

Now let's look at the most volatile running backs from 2014.

		Consistency	Receptions/Game
1	LeSean McCoy	31%	1.75
2	Shane Vereen	31%	3.25
3	Ryan Mathews	33%	1.50
4	Darren Sproles	40%	2.67
5	Andre Ellington	41%	3.83
6	Jonas Gray	42%	0.13
7	Marshawn Lynch	43%	2.31
8	Alfred Morris	43%	1.06
9	Rashad Jennings	45%	2.73
10	Jamaal Charles	45%	2.67
	Avg Rec/Game		2.29

Unsurprisingly, LeSean McCoy tops the charts. Even though he actually didn't have a horrible year overall, McCoy reached his salary-based expectation in just 31 percent of all games. A big part of the reason for that is probably due to Chip Kelly's offense, which didn't utilize Shady as a receiver out of the backfield; the back who never caught fewer than 40 passes in a year and once had 78 catches in a single season was held to only 28 catches in 2014—fewer than two per game.

Overall, this group contains primarily non-pass-catching backs. The average of 2.29 receptions per game would result in a 16-game total of just 37 catches, which would have ranked 23rd in the NFL for an individual running back. Only half of the backs surpassed 2.35 receptions per game.

With results this extreme, I think we have some solid evidence—not conclusive, but pretty strong—that pass-catching ability contributes to a running back's week-to-week volatility.

But what about upside? While it initially seems like backs who can score points in a variety of ways should possess the most upside, is that really the case? Here's a look at the top 10 backs in our Upside Rating, which measures how frequently a player reaches twice his salary-based expectation.

		Upside	Receptions/Game
1	Matt Asiata	50%	2.93
2	Jeremy Hill	31%	1.69
3	Jonathan Stewart	30%	1.92
4	Jonas Gray	28%	0.13
5	Tre Mason	25%	1.33
6	Ronnie Hillman	25%	2.63
7	Mark Ingram	23%	2.23
8	Branden Oliver	23%	2.57
9	C.J. Anderson	20%	2.27
10	Joique Bell	20%	2.27
		Avg Rec/Game	2.10

This group totaled only 2.1 receptions per game—even fewer than the bottom 10 in consistency. Not a single running back on this list managed even 3.0 receptions per game. It's littered with some pretty one-dimensional players—Jeremy Hill, Jonas Gray, Tre Mason, and Mark Ingram, especially—who rely pretty heavily on bulk attempts and touchdowns for their production.

I'm not saying pass-catching backs don't possess upside—they probably have more upside than non-pass-catching backs in a vacuum—but there's some evidence that non-pass-catchers have more upside (and less consistency) relative to their cost. Remember, all of our proprietary stats at Fantasy Labs are adjusted for historic pricing and production. Running backs who don't see a lot of targets cost less as a whole than pass-catchers, and if you're looking for pure upside per dollar, they're probably a superior bet to the pass-catchers.

None of this is evidence of a hard-and-fast rule like "Always start one-dimensional backs in tournaments," but I do think there's good reason to emphasize pass-catching ability in running backs when you want consistency—when you want to limit the range of outcomes for your lineup. And if you're going to go with a Jeremy Hill type of back in a cash game or when you otherwise want consistency, I'd do so only when his team is a heavy favorite; that skews the potential game flows toward those that are positive for that team's running back, limiting his downside exposure.

And just for fun (remember, I'm about as lame of a person as there is), I looked at overall running back consistency based on the Vegas lines. Running backs on teams favored by at least a touchdown had a Plus/Minus of 0.55 and a Consistency Rating of 39.6%. Those on teams that were at least a touchdown underdog had a Plus/Minus of -0.25 and a Consistency Rating of 35.9%.

In summation, pass-catching ability + being favored to win = good for consistency. No pass-catching ability + being the dog = bad for consistency.

Wide Receivers

Running backs have more week-to-week consistency than wide receivers. That's not true in every single instance—there are certain types of receivers who have more consistency than specific types of backs—but as a whole, running backs are more reliable over the course of a single game. That's due mostly to sample sizes; the top running backs see more than twice as many opportunities to touch the ball as the top wide receivers, and thus more chances for their production to regress toward the mean. There's simply less volatility on a weekly basis.

If consistency is at least partly a function of workload, we'd expect the most consistent wide receivers to be those who see the most targets, all else equal. Here's a look at the top 10 wide receivers from last year in terms of the Fantasy Labs Consistency Rating (frequency of games reaching their salary-based expectation).

		Consistency	Targets/Game
1	Odell Beckham	83%	10.83
2	Antonio Brown	75%	11.31
3	Allen Robinson	70%	8.10
4	Emmanuel Sanders	62%	8.81
5	Robert Woods	62%	6.50
6	Demaryius Thomas	62%	11.50
7	Greg Jennings	62%	5.75
8	Jarvis Landry	62%	7.00
9	Julian Edelman	61%	9.57
10	Julio Jones	60%	10.87
		Avg Targets/Game	**8.99**

Funny story. After Odell Beckham's Week 7 two-touchdown performance against the Cowboys, I tweeted something like "Anyone want to make a bet that Beckham won't score twice again this season?" Oh now wait, that's not funny at all.

That's actually completely idiotic. Beckham had three more multi-score games. No one took the bet, luckily.

Beckham is a freak and I missed on him, but surely part of his weekly consistency came because the Giants fed him the ball at a near-league-leading rate. We see other high-workload receivers on this list, too, including Antonio Brown, Demaryius Thomas, and Julio Jones.

Now let's take a look at the game's 10 least consistent wide receivers from last year.

		Consistency	Targets/Game
1	Josh Gordon	20%	9.40
2	Larry Fitzgerald	21%	7.36
3	Percy Harvin	23%	6.00
4	Pierre Garcon	25%	6.56
5	Calvin Johnson	30%	9.85
6	Vincent Jackson	31%	8.88
7	Michael Crabtree	31%	6.75
8	Victor Cruz	33%	6.83
9	Kenny Stills	33%	5.53
10	Kendall Wright	35%	6.64
		Avg Targets/Game	7.25

There's certainly still some studs here, but not a single receiver with double-digit targets per game. While only three of the top 10 most consistent receivers had fewer than eight targets per game, that number was seven of 10 for this list. Simply put, if you want receiver consistency on DraftKings, you need to emphasize opportunities.

Now, that might seem pretty obvious, but again, our Consistency Ratings are adjusted for cost. Wide receivers who see a lot of targets also cost a lot of money, but they're providing more consistency even after adjusting for that increased price tag.

The stat that I've been most excited to research in regards to wide receiver consistency is from Pro Football Focus: Mike Clay's aDOT, or Average Depth of Target. I've anecdotally found receivers who see shorter average targets to be more consistent, which is intuitively pretty logical; shorter targets lead to a higher catch rate, and thus a larger potential sample size of receptions. Basically, to predict wide receiver consistency, I think we need to examine both overall workload and the potential efficiency a receiver can generate with that workload. There's a reason that Vincent Jackson—a wide receiver who has historically relied on touchdowns and extremely long targets—has been one of the most volatile receivers ever on a weekly basis.

So here's a look at the aDOT for the top 10 most consistent receivers last year.

		Consistency	aDOT
1	Odell Beckham	83%	12.6
2	Antonio Brown	75%	10.4
3	Allen Robinson	70%	11.3
4	Emmanuel Sanders	62%	12.9
5	Robert Woods	62%	9.6
6	Demaryius Thomas	62%	10.5
7	Greg Jennings	62%	11.4
8	Jarvis Landry	62%	5.5
9	Julian Edelman	61%	7.6
10	Julio Jones	60%	12.4
		Avg aDOT	**10.42**

Overall, the most consistent receivers saw an average target length of 10.42 yards. We see a few notorious I-only-run-five-yards-downfield-and-then-turn-around receivers in Robert Woods, Jarvis Landry (are you serious with that aDOT bro?), and Julian Edelman. Further, Antonio Brown was the second-most consistent receiver in the NFL last year, and his targets are generally quite binary—either a quick screen or a pass deep down the field, and the abundance of the former ultimately makes Brown arguably the most long-term consistent wide receiver in NFL history.

Now let's examine the 10 least consistent receivers...

		Consistency	aDOT
1	Josh Gordon	20%	11.7
2	Larry Fitzgerald	21%	9.9
3	Percy Harvin	23%	10.4
4	Pierre Garcon	25%	10.2
5	Calvin Johnson	30%	16.3
6	Vincent Jackson	31%	15.3
7	Michael Crabtree	31%	9.0
8	Victor Cruz	33%	11.0
9	Kenny Stills	33%	12.8
10	Kendall Wright	35%	9.3
	Avg aDOT		11.59

There are three receivers in single-digits, and every one of them had absolutely horrific quarterback play that surely contributed to their inconsistencies. We also see two studs in Calvin Johnson and Vincent Jackson, both of whom saw a very large percentage of their targets come 10- and 20-plus yards downfield last year. Overall, these receivers had an aDOT that was 11 percent higher than the group of consistent receivers.

This all adds up to a pretty clear picture of the types of receivers who offer week-to-week consistency in the NFL: those with a large workload—especially on a PPR site like DraftKings—and preferably those who see a high frequency of short passes.

Quarterbacks

I've always been interested in the potential consistency of mobile passers. Just like pass-catching running backs, they have multiple ways to beat defenses—multiple means of scoring fantasy points to limit volatility. However, I've found problems with analyzing quarterbacks in terms of mobility because, frankly, so few of them run very much. Even Aaron Rodgers, whose mobility surely adds to his consistency and upside, is often among the league leaders in quarterback rushing and he still hasn't topped 269 yards in any of the past four seasons.

I never analyzed quarterbacks in terms of aDOT, but it should follow that the same relationship is there as it is with receivers; quarterbacks who chuck the ball downfield a lot (like Drew Stanton) should possess more weekly variance than those who get the ball out quickly underneath (like Tom Brady). To be clear, I have no idea how these numbers are going to turn out; it's just a theory and I really hope I don't have to delete all this stuff. I have things to do later tonight. Just kidding, I don't really have things to do, but I'd prefer not to be writing about quarterback volatility all day. Just kidding again, I wouldn't mind that.

#LadiesMan

So let's do this. The top 10 quarterbacks from last season in terms of consistency (minimum 13 DraftKings points per game)...

Okay, this is where I'm supposed to post the results, but the two numbers were basically exactly the same, so...shit. Told you I didn't look at anything beforehand. I'm a professional writer.

Moving on.

But for real, I can't really find any predictors of weekly consistency among quarterbacks. Not aDOT, not age, not salary. The one thing I will say is that quarterback consistency ratings as a whole are way higher than for other positions, which is the justification behind paying up for a quarterback in cash games; you know what you're getting more so than any other position.

Home vs Away (and a Trip to Vegas)

Players perform better at home. We know that, though *why* they're better is more challenging to isolate. It could be due to a lack of travel, maybe it's getting calls from refs, or perhaps it's the roar of the crowd. I don't know, I'm not a doctor, and I didn't stay at a Holiday Inn Express last night.

Whatever the reason, certain positions have a greater discrepancy than others when it comes to home versus road production. I took a look at the Plus/Minus for each position on DraftKings. Since Plus/Minus is cost-adjusted, this is basically a measure of how much DraftKings mispriced players based on game location. If the site perfectly accounted for home and road games, we'd see a Plus/Minus of 0.0 for each position.

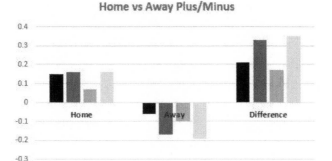

The biggest difference surprisingly comes at tight end, and I'm not sure why. Do teams utilize their tight ends more at home? Does DraftKings simply misprice tight ends more than other positions?

What's most interesting to me—and what makes the most intuitive sense—is the Plus/Minus differential for running backs. Running back production is often tied to game flow; home teams win the most, and thus are often leading late in games, allowing teams to keep the ball on the ground.

Part of what we're trying to capture here is a true home field advantage, but part of it is just the effect of good teams playing poor ones. We can use the Vegas lines to replicate that and predict game flow. We should naturally expect running backs to perform much better as favorites than as underdogs, then. What about all the positions?

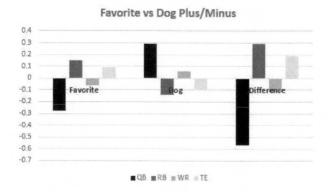

The positive bars in the "Difference" area (running backs and tight ends) are those positions that perform better as favorites, while the negative bars (quarterbacks and wide receivers) are those that perform better as underdogs.

Quarterback is the story here, as they gain nearly 0.6 expected points playing as underdogs. That's interesting since I've done work that suggests quarterback production itself "evens out," i.e. favorites and underdogs perform about the same overall. Since Plus/Minus is related to site pricing, that could be evidence that DraftKings is simply underpricing underdogs—mostly cheap quarterbacks. While I still prefer "overpaying" for top talent in cash games to mitigate risk, I do think there's a ton of value in finding a cheap quarterback with upside in GPPs.

And these differences are just for pure favorites and underdogs, which includes a lot of teams that are nearly evenly matched. If we include only -200 or better favorites and only +200 or worse underdogs, the quarterback Plus/Minus difference moves to 0.88 (in favor of being the underdog) and the running back Plus/Minus difference jumps to 0.81.

Vegas Totals and Position Value

There's a very clear linear relationship between Vegas totals and fantasy scoring in every sport. Baseball is the most closely linked due to the correlated play of the participants, but the link is strong in each game. That's not really surprising when you consider Vegas has more financial incentive than anyone to make accurate predictions; as much as people think they only care about balancing action, they make money (and limit their short-term downside) by first and foremost posting accurate lines.

I've showed in many of my past books how correlated NFL fantasy production is with the Vegas lines, but that doesn't mean the Vegas lines are automatically a perfect predictor of fantasy value. Remember, DFS sites aren't just pricing players randomly; even if they don't examine the Vegas odds, we'd still expect plenty of overlap between DraftKings player pricing and the projected Vegas totals, for example.

So how well does DraftKings account for game totals, and are there any areas we can exploit? I used the Trends tool at Fantasy Labs to look up the historic Plus/Minus (actual production minus salary-based expected production) for players in games with varying Vegas totals (sorted into three buckets). For the record, I looked at closing totals.

	Plus/Minus Based on Vegas Total		
	<43	43-50	>50
QB	0.73	-0.26	0.97
RB	0.04	-0.14	0.6
WR	0.07	-0.02	0.13
TE	0.25	-0.09	0.13

This is pretty interesting. Every single position has seen a positive value in games with either a very low total (fewer than 43 projected points) or a high total (over 50 points). On the flip side, every position had a negative Plus/Minus in games with a middle-of-the-pack Vegas total of between 43 and 50 points.

The Plus/Minus for games with a high total isn't surprising. Even with DraftKings compensating by pricing players higher in those games, there's still meat left on the bone; they aren't pricing players (quarterbacks and running backs, in particular) in those games as high as they should be.

However, the value that we've seen for players in games with a very low projected total is more perplexing. My guess is it's just an overreaction to two poor teams facing off. I don't think this is reason to specifically target players in Browns-Jaguars games, but perhaps there's also no reason to avoid a quality player who will see a heavy workload if he's in a low-projected game. Basically, you're trading in some expected fantasy production on the team level for a larger individual market share of that production; 50% of 50 team points is better than 20% of 100 team points.

It's also very possible that this is just evidence of the two extremes of pricing being off. DraftKings doesn't necessarily have a pricing ceiling, but they probably aren't going to price a quarterback at $14,000 when everyone else is at $10,000, even if it were justified. They have to be concerned not only with accuracy, but also creating prices that won't create insane lineup overlap—thus, perhaps, the value that's apparent at the pricing extremes.

Whatever the case, I think what we've established is that the fantasy production at certain positions correlates better with the Vegas odds. Wide receivers produce nearly equally in almost any situation, whereas there seem to be great pricing inefficiencies on running backs (perhaps due to mid-week injuries) and quarterbacks.

Division vs. Non-Division Games

I believe Robert Griffin III had the best rookie season for any player in NFL history. The guy was absolutely insane. He averaged 8.14 yards per attempt, turned in a 4-to-1 touchdown-to-interception ratio, posted a 102.4 passer rating, and oh yeah, he also ran for 815 yards and seven touchdowns. Dafuq? My favorite stat from RGIII's rookie year is that he had the highest-ever passer rating against the blitz. Not for a rookie—for any quarterback in NFL history. That's bananas.

Since that 2012 rookie season, Griffin has been...okay. I don't think he's been as poor as a lot of people think—his rookie year set the bar so high that he was bound to underachieve relative to expectations—but RGIII certainly hasn't been able to recapture the magic of 2012. Injuries are certainly part of the equation there, but I also think there's an element of familiarity; RGIII and similar quarterbacks have been able to parlay their unique skill sets into success very early in their careers, but many have either regressed or flatlined after their initial breakouts.

We've seen the same sort of thing happen with Colin Kaepernick (career-best numbers almost across the board in his first full season), Cam Newton (basically the exact same season for four consecutive years, albeit with absolutely no help offensively), and Nick Foles (arguably the most efficient season ever with 27 touchdowns and two picks in 2013 to a 13-to-10 ratio in 2014).

I really believe there's something to be said for defenses "figuring out" these passers. The majority of a defensive coordinator's job comes down to "let's make it really difficult for the other team to throw the football," and that was especially true as coaches zeroed in on stopping RGIII & Co.

I bring this up because I think we see a similar phenomenon in division games; heading into the 2013 season, for example, you can bet Philly, Dallas, and New York were pissing their pants about Griffin's upside in Washington. They likely spent a whole lot of time preparing to face him. And even if they just did normal prep, that's twice as much time as non-division teams that faced RGIII just once in 2013.

So what are the numbers on fantasy production in division games? Do defenses really adjust when facing an offense twice? Let's view it through the lens of DraftKings Plus/Minus.

	Division	Non-Division
QB	-0.72	0.46
RB	0.01	-0.01
WR	-0.25	0.15
TE	-0.14	0.08

Historically, running backs have offered around the same amount of value whether playing in or out of the division. Pass-catchers have been a bit superior out of the division—bordering on significant results—but look at quarterbacks; there's an expected difference of 1.18 DraftKings points when a quarterback is playing a division foe as opposed to someone outside of the division. That's huge, especially since we're considering *all* division games.

So what if we separate this a bit, looking at trends over time? Here's how quarterbacks fared in division games last season...

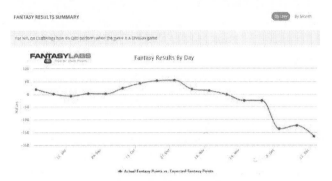

This is really interesting. From Week 1 to Week 12 of last season, quarterbacks in division games hovered around a neutral Plus/Minus, i.e. they were more or less priced accurately. Then, over the final five weeks of the regular season, these quarterbacks collectively performed over 150 points below expectations. The drop was a steep one.

At first I thought this might be due to weather. Precipitation, strong winds, and cold temperatures affect passing efficiency (and cause coaches to call fewer pass plays, too), so maybe DraftKings just doesn't alter their pricing to account for changes in passing stats late in the year.

So I looked at quarterbacks in non-division games...

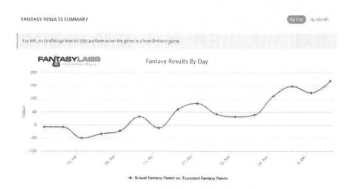

FANTASY RESULTS SUMMARY

For NFL on DraftKings how do QBs perform when the game is a Non-Division game

Fantasy Results By Day

◆ Actual Fantasy Points vs. Expected Fantasy Points

Um, yeahhhh. So it isn't weather-related. So quarterbacks perform worse in division games late in the year, and it isn't due to weather—perhaps a sign that defenses "catch up" and are better prepared to stop an offense's signal-caller after already seeing him once in a year.

To me, this is very actionable information due to how extreme the results are and how much it makes sense intuitively. With any theory and accompanying data, we want it to fit with common sense. If it doesn't, that's fine, but then we need more overwhelming statistical proof that what we used to believe is wrong. In this case, everything meshes with the idea that quarterbacks are better out of the division than in it, especially in the second intra-division meeting of the season.

The Importance of Workload for Quarterbacks

DeSean Jackson had 1,169 yards and six touchdowns last season. Anquan Boldin had a comparable 1,062 yards and five scores, but it took him 27 more catches than Jackson to reach those lesser numbers. D-Jax averaged a league-high 20.9 yards per reception—63 percent higher than Boldin's 12.8.

For wide receivers, efficiency is really important. Based on their skill set, wide receivers can have drastically different yards per reception. They also differ quite a bit in terms of red zone scoring efficiency. For the epitome of how efficiency can sometimes trump workload for receivers, look no further than Martavis Bryant's 2014 rookie season.

Quarterbacks aren't like that. There's not a massive deviation in their efficiency. Last season, Tony Romo led the NFL with 8.5 yards per attempt, but that was only 21 percent better than the league's 25th ranked passer in Nick Foles. Meanwhile, Drew Brees led the league in passing attempts at 659, and that was 80 percent higher than the 25th-ranked quarterback (Geno Smith).

Of course, DraftKings accounts for expected workload to an extent with their pricing. So how much value is left?

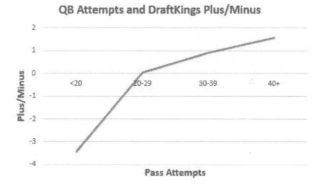

There's a clear relationship here; more attempts is always better, obviously, but it isn't until around the 30-attempt range that quarterbacks have tended to offer value over their cost. It is critical to get exposure to those players. Let's compare these numbers to quarterback efficiency and daily fantasy value.

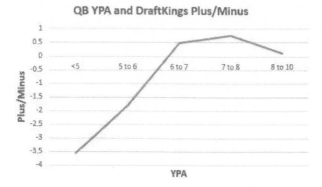

It's pretty critical that your quarterback doesn't completely tank, obviously, but once you hit around the 6.0 YPA mark—and that isn't a quality number for a passer—value starts to even out. Part of that is because, when a quarterback is really efficient early in a game, he generally won't be throwing a lot of passes in that game; he cannibalizes his own fantasy upside because, unless the other quarterback is rolling and the game turns into a shootout, it's tough to be both super-efficient and throw the ball a whole lot.

The point is that with quarterbacks, anticipated workload is the first and most important thing to consider. You absolutely need to get exposure to quarterbacks who are going to air the ball out early and often, then try to figure out which of those are going to be the most efficient.

Top Performers in 2014

My goal with the majority of the data in this book is to provide actionable tools—numbers you can ultimately utilize to help you make money. Once in a while, though, I think it's just fun to look at past stats and leaderboards. I do think some of the data in this section is actionable—most of it on the position level—but here are some individual stats from

2014 that I think are pretty interesting as well. First, the most ridiculous of numbers...

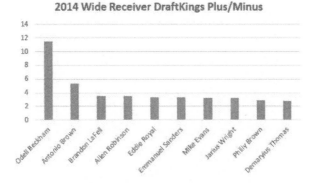

You're looking at the Fantasy Labs Plus/Minus stats for last season's wide receivers. Remember, this is actual points minus salary-based expected points. Can you spot which one of those players doesn't look like the others?

Obviously Odell Beckham turned in one of the great rookie season ever. I do think this chart is more explanatory than predictive—it just shows us that ODB was really freakin' good and also didn't cost much for a little while—but there are more useful insights if we study positional Plus/Minus.

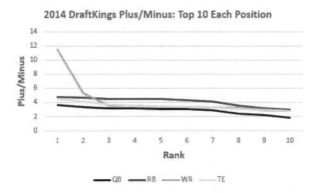

You can see Beckham was an outlier not only at wide receiver, but also just as a fantasy asset in general. His Plus/Minus was more than double that of any other player in the NFL last season. Bananas.

Even though Beckham was a freak, I still think there was a good probability of a wide receiver leading the league in Plus/Minus; the No. 2 overall player was also a wide receiver in Antonio Brown. That's because wide receivers are high-variance plays on a weekly basis and there are a bunch of them, so just by chance alone, we'd probably expect some to overachieve even over the course of an entire season.

I also think it's interesting that quarterbacks posted the lowest Plus/Minus numbers across the board; the top quarterback in Plus/Minus (Ben Roethlisberger) was right around as valuable as the No. 8 running back (Jonathan Stewart).

Here's a look at the results by name.

	Quarterbacks	Running Backs	Wide Receivers	Tight Ends
1	Ben Roethlisberger	Matt Asiata	Odell Beckham	Jermaine Gresham
2	Teddy Bridgewater	C.J. Anderson	Antonio Brown	Charles Clay
3	Russell Wilson	Ronnie Hillman	Brandon LaFell	Coby Fleener
4	Derek Carr	Le'Veon Bell	Allen Robinson	Marcedes Lewis
5	Mark Sanchez	Jeremy Hill	Eddie Royal	Travis Kelce
6	Ryan Fitzpatrick	Jonas Gray	Emmanuel Sanders	Mychal Rivera
7	Andrew Luck	Ahmad Bradshaw	Mike Evans	Antonio Gates
8	Kyle Orton	Jonathan Stewart	Jarius Wright	Scott Chandler
9	Aaron Rodgers	DeMarco Murray	Philly Brown	Zach Ertz
10	Drew Stanton	Justin Forsett	Demaryius Thomas	Jared Cook

We see a few names at each position that were decent fantasy commodities that mostly just overachieved relative to their cost (Derek Carr, Ryan Fitzpatrick, Matt Asiata, Jonas Gray, Allen Robinson, and so on). There are some studs at the first three positions, but a lack of top-flight talent at tight end. Even though I don't want to draw too many conclusions from these lists, I do think there's perhaps something to the idea that the top tight ends not named Rob Gronkowski were overpriced last year. Whereas I liked a double-tight-end strategy in GPPs the prior season, it really didn't work out last year; Gronk is a beast, but the other tight ends just don't have enough upside to merit use in the flex at their current prices (sans perhaps Jimmy Graham given his scoring ability in certain matchups).

"Often the difference between a successful man and a failure is not one's better abilities or ideas, but the courage that one has to bet on his ideas, to take a calculated risk, and to act."

Maxwell Maltz

IV. A Numbers Game: The Data on What's Really Winning Leagues

"You have to learn the rules of the game. And then you have to play better than anyone else."

Albert Einstein

One of my favorite parts of Fantasy Labs is the sheer amount of data we offer. We combine historic salary and performance data with everything from Vegas lines to stat splits to weather information, then let you play around with all of it to test theories and create models.

But there are certain pieces of data we just don't have right now. I was lucky enough to once again partner with DraftKings to get answers to a bunch of questions I (and a lot of you) have been wondering.

What are the optimal stacks to use? How much do ownership rates affect GPP win rates? Which positions are best for use in the flex? How much stiffer does the competition get at higher stakes?

Now we have answers.

Average NFL Scores

Whenever I do any sort of research for one of my books, readers always ask me if I can uncover the average scores on <u>DraftKings</u>. So here you go.

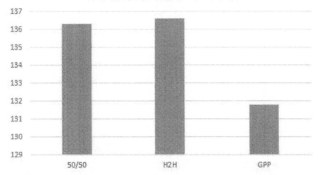

I think these exact numbers don't really matter much; does knowing you need around 136 points to cash in the average 50/50 as opposed to, say, 140 points, change the way you approach it? Probably not.

What is interesting is how the average scores compare for each league type. I figured 50/50s might be slightly tougher overall, but that might not be the case. Now, they could indeed be more volatile (in a couple ways, one of which is if quality players enter the same lineup into them a bunch), but the average score is just slightly lower than in head-to-heads.

Here's how things break down by stakes...

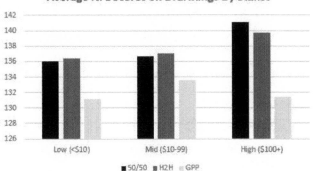

While head-to-head scoring outpaces 50/50 scoring in low and mid-stakes games, it's a bit higher at higher stakes. Again, I think this is probably due to top players being more willing to multi-enter really high-quality lineups, pushing up the average score a bit. It could also be the case that fish are more likely to play a single heads-up game and hope to get lucky than they are to try the same in a 50/50—where one crap lineup from a single opponent doesn't help all that much.

What's interesting is that the average cash game scores in low-stakes leagues (below $10) are roughly the same as those in mid-stakes leagues (between $10 and $99). The average score soars at higher stakes, unsurprisingly, but this data lends credence to the idea that NFL games at moderate stakes have plenty of weak players and are probably much more beatable than high-stakes games. This isn't the same for other sports, so my guess is DraftKings' ability to acquire new customers in abundance during the NFL season keeps even the mid-stakes games pretty "fishy."

Finally, you can see GPP scores are far lower than cash games at all levels. This isn't a surprise at all since even casual players understand GPP play is less about being price-sensitive and seeking value than cash games.

However, it's pretty surprising to see high-stakes GPPs with roughly the same average score as low-stakes tournaments. I think this could potentially be due to sharks and whales being more inclined to multi-enter GPPs, diversifying their lineups much more than in cash games and ultimately forgoing value, but I can't be sure. It's worth noting the average cashing score in high-stakes GPPs is just 164.5 points—a full two points lower than in low-stakes GPPs.

I'm not going to draw any firm conclusions here; you can make of these numbers what you will.

Salary Cap Allocation

I wrote an NFL book a couple years ago that displayed the typical salary cap distribution for average and winning teams, and a bunch of people seemed to rush to build lineups with players whose prices matched up with those numbers.

DON'T DO THAT!

Every week is different, and it would be foolish to not play the best value just because he has a certain price. However, I do think there's value in analyzing salary cap allocation data in two ways. The first is determining if you're consistently overpaying or underpaying at a position. If you analyze all of your lineups from last season and see you're spending $1,000 less on quarterbacks than the typical winning lineup, you probably need to take a look at that. The value is over the long run.

The other way—the real value, in my view—is comparing cashing to non-cashing lineups. How are the best lineups allocating their cap space? How is that different from what the average player is doing? Here's a look at the average salaries for cash-game lineups on DraftKings last season...

Salary Cap Allocation in Cash Games			
Position	Non-Cashing Lineups	Cashing Lineups	% Change
QB	$7,361	$7,379	0.24%
RB	$14,915	$15,125	1.41%
WR	$19,288	$19,257	-0.16%
TE	$5,239	$5,050	-3.61%
DST	$3,069	$3,087	0.59%

On average, winning cash lineups spend a little more money on quarterbacks and defenses and a lot more money on running backs. The quarterback and running back numbers are unsurprising given what we know about the position volatility; as the most consistent positions on a weekly basis, it's smart to find reliable, elite production out of your quarterback and running backs.

Defense is a little bit trickier, but I suspect there's more predictability on a weekly basis than most realize. It's common knowledge that defenses are volatile—and they are to an extent—but it's not like there's zero week-to-week predictability. It's just a matter of whether or not the distribution of defense salaries—how much it costs to roster a top one or even an average one compared to the price of a cheap one—matches up with that predictability.

Still, I wouldn't break the bank at defense. My guess is this data is reflective of poor fantasy players being willing to roster really shitty defenses because they've heard it's completely random. I think a generally smart cash-game strategy is to find a relatively cheap defense—if there is one—that is going to be able to get to the quarterback (and is preferably playing one likely to give away the football when pressured).

Wide receiver and tight end are the two positions at which winning lineups spent less than losing ones. Again, this is understandable given the variance at the position. The wide receiver numbers are more or less even, though, while tight end really stands out, with cashing lineups spending 3.61 percent less than non-cashing ones, on average. Part of the effect is likely due to how some top tight ends performed last year, but the idea that you should generally save on tight ends in cash games holds water. Are there times when Gronk is underpriced and worthy of consideration? Of course, but you shouldn't be consistently building your cash lineups around an expensive tight end.

Of course, we all know GPPs are a different animal. How does tournament salary cap allocation compare to that in cash games?

Salary Cap Allocation in GPPs			
Position	Non-Cashing Lineups	Cashing Lineups	% Change
QB	$7,425	$7,363	-0.84%
RB	$14,010	$13,928	-0.59%
WR	$20,083	$20,377	1.46%
TE	$5,272	$5,141	-2.48%
DST	$3,066	$3,069	0.10%

Unlike in cash games, winning GPP teams spent less on quarterbacks and running backs and more on wide receivers. Again, this makes intuitive sense; the former two spots possess the least weekly volatility, while receivers are highly variable from game to game—a good thing to embrace in tournaments.

It's interesting to see tight ends again in the gutter. Again, part of it is simply due to a down season for the position as a whole. And at this point, tight end seems to be a pay-for-Gronk-or-punt sort of position. That could change, but I'm generally one to favor tight ends at one end of the salary cap spectrum or the other.

What's really interesting is how the numbers on winning lineups for cash games compare to those in GPPs. Check this out…

Position	Cash Winners	GPP Winners	% Change
QB	$7,379	$7,363	-0.22%
RB	$15,125	$13,928	-7.91%
WR	$19,257	$20,377	5.82%
TE	$5,050	$5,141	1.80%
DST	$3,087	$3,069	-0.58%

Winning GPP lineups are spending a tad less on quarterbacks, a little bit more on tight ends, and a few bucks less on defenses. But take a look at running backs and wide receivers.

With just a $50,000 cap, last year's winning GPP lineups spent an average of $1,197 less on running backs than winning cash lineups. That's insane. If you can hit on an underpriced running back—especially one who isn't widely utilized—it really opens up a lot of cap flexibility.

And much of that extra cap space should probably go to wide receivers. I absolutely love "overpaying" for elite receivers in decent or even perceived poor matchups, and top GPP lineups seem to be willing to spend big at the position.

At the end of the day, elite wide receivers just have so much upside, and you want to give yourself as much GPP exposure to those high-ceiling players as you can. Upside can be manufactured for running backs in the form of bulk attempts, while wide receiver upside is much more dependent on a combination of targets and an elite skill set—something for which you need to pay.

Stacking in NFL

In the beginning of this book, I showed some data on the correlation between each offensive position. I think that's extremely useful information when creating lineups because correlated production is arguably the most overlooked aspect of giving yourself exposure to desired outcomes. Even if utilizing players with correlated production doesn't alter your median projection—which it can in the case of traditional QB-WR stacks—it does alter the probability of scoring in certain ranges.

I think it's so important to build lineups in a smart way with correlated production that I believe two players could use the exact same set of player projections and one could be long-term profitable over the other just from being smart with lineup construction. It matters a lot.

Thanks to DraftKings, we can look at both the popularity and value of certain lineup combinations in both cash games and GPPs...

	H2H + 50/50		GPPs	
	Usage	Cashing	Usage	Cashing
QB + RB + WR	5.5%	43.0%	9.0%	19.3%
QB + RB[1]	8.0%	50.6%	7.3%	19.9%
QB + WR[1]	32.5%	48.6%	38.4%	22.0%
QB + 2 WR[1]	2.4%	47.2%	4.3%	21.6%
WR + RB[2]	22.8%	51.3%	22.1%	20.4%
QB + WR + TE	3.1%	42.2%	6.0%	20.9%
QB + 3 Receivers[3]	0.6%	48.8%	1.1%	19.4%
RB + D	18.4%	52.2%	17.2%	21.4%
None of the Above	29.6%	52.8%	23.3%	20.8%

A few notes regarding the chart...

1) Mutually exclusive from QB + RB + WR

2) With no stacked QB

3) At least one receiver is a tight end

There's so much data here and so many things to discuss. I'm just going to take it stack by stack.

Stack by stack, day by day.
A fresh start over, a different hand to play.
The deeper we fall, the stronger we stay.
And we'll be better...
The second time around.

K. Moving on.

QB + RB + WR

DraftKings users stacked a quarterback, running back, and wide receiver from the same team in 5.5 percent of cash games and 9.0 percent of GPPs last year. It was a losing strategy in both, winning at just a 43.0 percent clip in cash games—which is horrendous given a random expectation of 50.0 percent—and cashing at just a 19.3 percent rate in GPPs. No stack studied won a lower rate of GPPs.

Why? Well, in stacking three players from the same team, you're obviously taking on some risk. If the offense tanks, you're done. It's simply too much risk in cash games, and that 43.0 percent win rate is glaring evidence that's indeed the case.

In tournaments, you obviously get the upside of a quarterback and wide receiver pairing, but adding in a running back has the opposite effect. On most teams, running backs cannibalize points from the receivers, and vice versa; every wide receiver reception and touchdown is a lack of scoring for the running back.

Further, game flow generally forces teams into an end-game strategy that emphasizes either the passing game or the running game, not both. There might be certain backs who benefit from being down in the game and can thus be considered as part of a QB-RB-WR stack—Shane Vereen with Eli Manning and Odell Beckham, for example. For the most part, though, this is a combination we see in nearly 1-in-10 tournament lineups that I really don't like.

QB + RB

If we remove the wide receiver from the equation—a strategy I've seen quite a bit in cash games to capitalize on the upside of a potent offense, regardless of whether they're winning or losing—cash game success jumps quite a bit to a 50.6 percent win rate. I don't think that's stellar by any means, but it's slightly better than average. Assuming the offense stacked is selected in an intelligent manner, I think that baseline can increase more, too. While I don't go out of my way to stack a quarterback and running back in cash games, I don't think it needs to be avoided, either.

In GPPs, the case rate falls a tad below average. It's interesting that QB/RB has performed better than QB/RB/WR in tournaments, although the difference is small, and I'd guess there's a selection bias in favor of serious pass-catching running backs when a user stacks a quarterback and running back together in a tournament. But again, I'm not going out of my way to do it, particularly because I think you use a lot of the double-touchdown upside you can get by stacking a receiver with your quarterback.

QB + WR

Stacking a single wide receiver with his quarterback is the most popular tournament pairing, by far, with 38.4 percent usage. That's unsurprising given that the public is obviously aware of the upside of stacking. And overall, no combination of teammates has led to a higher GPP cash rate—22.0 percent.

What's shocking to me, however, is that nearly just as many lineups—32.5 percent—used a QB/WR pairing in cash games. It seems the public has either 1) mistakenly applied a general GPP strategy to cash games, which is probably the case with most, or 2) bet on the upside of stacking outweighing the risk.

The truth is that stacking a wide receiver with a quarterback very clearly improves upside, but there's a lot of risk you're taking on, too, hence the low 48.6 percent win rate in cash games (but 22.0 percent cash rate in tournaments). I've done a lot of research on this topic because doing fun shit on Friday and Saturday nights isn't really my thang.

Take a look at how often quarterbacks and wide receivers have top games together...

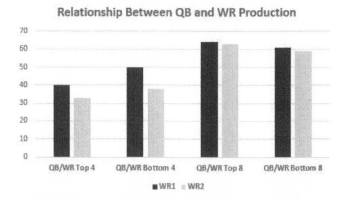

If production weren't correlated, we'd expect quarterbacks to have a top-four performance on the season in 25 percent of the games their WR1 had the same. It's actually 40 percent, which is good and shows correlation. But their poor games— a bottom-four performance—sync up half the time, which is double the random expectation.

Every situation is different. There are times when I'm okay stacking a quarterback and wide receiver in cash games—I've done it quite a bit with Tom Brady and Julian Edelman due to the nature of their games—but overall, it's a lot of risk to take on for (probably) less upside.

QB + 2WR

When we talk about stacking in daily fantasy football, it's not truly stacking an entire offense in the same way as in baseball. In baseball, there's no limit to how much teammates can score. A hit for one batter is always a positive thing for his teammates.

Football is like a combination of baseball and basketball—a sport in which, for the most part, teammates cannibalize one another. There are some synergistic situations in basketball with assists, but for the most part, points for one player mean a lack of points for his teammates.

We've already seen a bit of the cannibalizing effect with wide receivers and running backs, to an extent, and we obviously have positively correlated play with quarterbacks and wide receivers. But how much is too much? Obviously pairing a quarterback with his top three receivers and tight end is overdoing it—football is a timed game and there's only so much upside to go around—but is utilizing two receivers with their quarterback worth it?

I think the general consensus in the past has been that it isn't. Anecdotally, I never seemed to see many QB/WR/WR stacks out there. That fits with the data, as just 2.4 percent of cash lineups and 4.3 percent of GPP lineups utilized the combination. In cash games, there's good reason for it—a lot of risk, which has led to a 47.2 percent win rate.

In tournaments, though, I think there's good reason to reconsider the QB/WR/WR stack. First of all, it has led to a 21.6 percent cash rate, which is the second-best of any player combination. Further, I think you can probably increase that baseline by sticking to offenses projected really well by Vegas to ensure there's plenty of scoring to go around.

Second, no one is using it! With fewer than one-in-20 GPP lineups using QB/WR/WR, it's actually a contrarian stack when it shouldn't be. I think you could make an argument that stacking a quarterback from an explosive offense with two of his receivers is the most underutilized and potentially most +EV tournament move you could make. There's serious upside here.

WR + RB

The wide receiver and running back combination studied included only those without a quarterback in the mix. I was surprised to see that 22.8 percent of all cash lineups last year utilized this combination, which means daily fantasy players love to buy in on certain offenses, even in head-to-heads and 50/50s. And it led to a 51.3 percent cash rate, which is pretty good.

The combination was also popular in tournaments, although just moderately successful. I'm not a huge fan of the strategy in GPPs because I think it limits your true upside, for reasons already explained. Plus, you aren't even getting the upside from a quarterback/wide receiver combination. It might help you cash, but not win. And if you look at the numbers, the WR/RB combination won only 0.006 percent of all GPPs last year—despite being utilized often—and that number was the second-worst of any position combination.

With top-heavy payouts, the goal going into any tournament should be to win it, not simply to cash. I can't imagine it's +EV to give yourself little exposure to those top payouts, even if you have a decent probability of cashing. Except in rare instances, this combination isn't for me.

QB + WR + TE

For the most part, this stack is similar to QB/WR/WR, with potentially greater scoring upside. With just a 42.2 percent cash rate in head-to-head and 50/50 games and the known volatility of tight ends, I'd pretty much never use this combination in cash games.

In tournaments, though, I think you can again be contrarian by "double-stacking" receivers with your quarterback. The cash rate is good, and a QB/WR/TE stack actually won 0.021 percent of the time it was used, which was the highest rate of any single stack last year. Again, if your goal is to win a tournament, I love pairing a quarterback with two of his pass-catchers.

QB + 3 Receivers

So how far is too far? Is there possibly enough upside to go around for three pass-catchers? As you'd probably guess, no. Using three receivers (at least one of which is a tight end) has led to below-average cash rates in both cash games and GPPs. Even with high-upside offenses, it's not a strategy I'd recommend in any format.

RB + D

The idea behind pairing a running back with his defense is that, if the defense performs well, the team is probably winning the game, in which case the running back should see a heavier workload. I think it's also a fairly low-risk combination because there's nothing to say either a running back or defense can't perform well even if the other doesn't.

And overall, a RB/D combination has led to above-average success in both cash games and GPPs. One thing I'll mention is I think you should generally be pairing the two together when the team is a favorite to win, especially if you plan to use it in a cash game. Using Marshawn Lynch with the Seattle defense can be a potent strategy in most games, but if the

Seahawks are dogs, Lynch becomes way more fragile of a play.

The other thing to consider is this correlation is probably much stronger for non-pass-catching backs. A player like Matt Forte arguably becomes better if his defense performs worse since he might see more targets. That's why I generally prefer pass-catching backs in cash games and might take a chance on a Lynch-esque back with his defense in GPPs.

No Stack

Of all the different combinations of teammates you can put into your lineup, it's not pairing anyone that has actually led to the most success in cash games with a baseline win rate of 52.8 percent. I certainly think you can find smart ways to stack, even in cash, but overall, most of the time the risk probably outweighs the reward. Fewer than one in three cash lineups didn't stack at all last season.

In tournaments, I think not stacking is similar to using a wide receiver and running back together in that you might have a decent shot to cash, but you're not maximizing your win probability. Like WR/RB, no stack led to just a 0.006 percent win rate in GPPs, which is poor.

I think there's a decent case to be made to forgo stacking in baseball, which is ironic given that the correlations in that sport are even stronger than in football. However, whereas stacking in baseball creates massive lineup overlap, that's not necessarily the case in daily fantasy football. I think you can easily stack—even the chalk—and still be contrarian, and the upside stacking provides is well worth the risk in tournaments.

Ownership, Cashing, and Winning GPPs

I'm a big believer in the wisdom of the crowd. Everyone has their own biases, but those tend to get muted over large samples. Assuming there isn't massive overlap in opinions, the collection of expert rankings should beat the majority of those experts taken in isolation over the long run.

The daily fantasy market as a whole gets it at least partially right, too. The players in the most lineups generally score the most points. Here's a look at average points scored sorted by ownership. The first row is the top quarter of all players in terms of ownership, the second is the next bucket, and so on.

Avg. Score	QB	RB	WR	TE	DST
1st	19.3	14.2	15.1	10.5	9.2
2nd	16.9	8.0	9.9	5.8	7.6
3rd	15.5	4.6	4.8	3.9	6.8
4th	7.5	3.1	3.2	2.9	6.4

Every single descending ownership bucket sees fewer points than the one before it, i.e. the top-owned quarterbacks score more than the next tier of quarterbacks, who score more than the next, and so on. There's no point at which ownership is totally inefficient. This suggests the most popular plays are also the highest-value plays. But how much incentive is there to side with the crowd at each position?

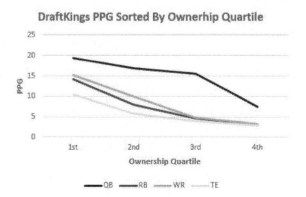

DraftKings PPG Sorted By Ownerhip Quartile

Running back, wide receiver, and tight end are all roughly the same in terms of how ownership affected projected output. All see large drops from the first to the second and second to the third ownership quartiles.

Meanwhile, quarterback production is somewhat flat across the first three ownership buckets. For example, the top 25 percent of running backs in terms of ownership score 14.2 points, while the next 25 percent score 8.0 points—a difference of 6.2 points. Meanwhile, the top bucket of quarterbacks checks in at 19.3 points and the next is at 16.9 points—a difference of only 2.4 points.

Some of that is due to the depth at each position, but we even see a larger drop at tight end. In effect, this represents the scarcity at each position, fitting with the "late-round quarterback" theory from the season-long fantasy football realm that quarterbacks are somewhat replaceable if you're smart about it.

Now, don't forget we're dealing with median points and not consistency or other important factors—which does increase the value of elite quarterbacks in cash games—but I definitely think there's something useful here.

Although ownership is generally considered to be more important in tournament play, I actually think it has immense value in cash games, too. If you can accurately predict ownership, whether it's by looking at early lineups or even just aggregating expert rankings, you can probably create profitable (and extremely chalky) cash lineups. There are exceptions, but I think the crowd as a whole generally gets it right with ownership in cash games. Remember, I'm more bullish on the long-term profitability of GPPs than cash games, and this is one reason why; cash games are more easily solved.

In tournaments, we're talking about a totally different strategy. Ownership matters because you generally want to differentiate yourself in some manner. Whereas lineup overlap doesn't hurt you (or at least not in a big way) in cash games, it can have a monumental impact on GPP success.

Thus, we're better off viewing how ownership affects actual GPP win rates than total points. Here's a look at lineups sorted into 10 buckets based on ownership, how often they cashed, and what percentage of tournaments wins they generated...

DraftKings GPP Ownership			
Ownership Decile	Avg Player Ownership	% Cashing	Share of Wins
1st	18.56%	29.0%	11.6%
2nd	15.22%	24.7%	5.8%
3rd	13.78%	23.1%	11.6%
4th	12.67%	22.0%	10.1%
5th	11.78%	21.0%	20.3%
6th	10.89%	19.8%	7.2%
7th	10.11%	18.6%	10.1%
8th	9.22%	17.5%	2.9%
9th	8.11%	16.4%	10.1%
10th	6.22%	14.2%	10.1%

The top decile of lineups in terms of ownership saw a typical player in 18.56 percent of lineups, cashed 29.0 percent of the time, and won a total of 11.6 percent of all GPPs. We'd obviously expect 10.0 percent based on randomness alone, so the GPP win rate is just a tad above average.

The cash rate trend is pretty amazing...

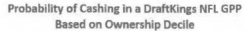

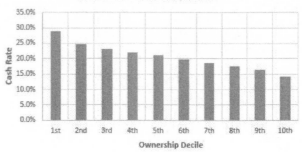

Not only do high-ownership lineups lead to the most points, but they also maximize the chances of cashing. Playing the chalk increases your chances of cashing in a tournament, while being contrarian lowers it. I don't think this is overly surprising, but it does suggest the public is somewhat efficient and that being contrarian is truly an all-or-nothing type of strategy.

If you notice, though, the rates of GPP wins are all over the place. Here's the relationship between ownership and GPP win share...

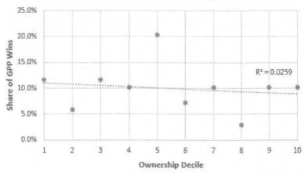

With an r-value of 0.0259, there's only a very weak positive relationship between ownership and tournament win probability. I think the individual decile results are fairly noisy, but this trendline shows a general lack of a relationship.

Actually, if you throw out the bottom 30 percent of ownership deciles—generally filled with mostly low-value plays—you'd see a negative correlation between ownership and win rates, i.e. as ownership decreases, GPP win probability increases.

Last year, the middle-of-the-pack players in terms of ownership led to around a 20 percent higher GPP probability than teams in the top 30 percent in cumulative ownership. And that's with those top teams scoring more points. To reiterate, here's the average winning GPP score charted against cumulative ownership.

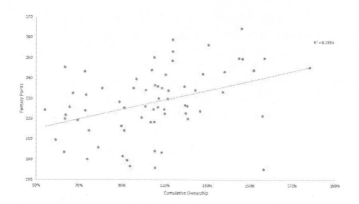

The higher the average ownership of your lineup, the more points they'll score. That does not mean we should necessarily be chasing points at all costs. If ownership didn't matter at all, we'd see the ownership vs. GPP success data look a lot different.

We're really in a bit of a pickle with GPP strategy. With an antifragile approach, you should be trying to win without needing to score a shit-ton of points to do it. When you roster the chalk, as you can see in the previous graph, you basically force yourself into needing to be perfect. I'd much rather need to score 200 points to win a GPP than be required to hit 250 or something ridiculous.

What this data tells me is this:

1) You shouldn't always be rostering the chalk because it almost always requires a higher threshold of scoring to win.

2) You shouldn't always be super-contrarian because, well, high-ownership players are in a lot of lineups for a reason; they typically offer a lot of value that you must forgo if you want to get away from the chalk.

3) You really need to balance lineups with obvious values and under-the-radar plays, emphasizing low-ownership players

139 | P a g e

whenever a popular player isn't a clear value; if the values are close for me between a chalk play and a contrarian one, I'm sure as shit playing the latter.

4) When you really like a player you believe won't be in a lot of lineups, you should utilize him as a foundational tournament piece. Building around those players—ones you think are both high-value and low-ownership—is how tournaments are won.

Highest Usage and Cash Rates

My hope is that you find the majority of the data and information in this book to be predictive and actionable. The following is probably not that, but I still think it's pretty fun to look at which players were in the most lineups and which guys led to the most success. Let's start with the most popular players in last year's cash games...

Most Popular Players in DraftKings Cash Games			
Name	Position	% Used	Cash %
Le'Veon Bell	RB	17.55%	57%
LeSean McCoy	RB	17.01%	50%
Jordy Nelson	WR	16.65%	61%
Kelvin Benjamin	WR	15.57%	53%
Jeremy Hill	RB	15.30%	65%
CJ Anderson	RB	14.31%	64%
Antonio Brown	WR	13.59%	55%
Julio Jones	WR	13.14%	49%
Rob Gronkowski	TE	11.97%	55%
Broncos	DST	11.16%	55%

Le'Veon Bell leading the way isn't a surprise, but Shady McCoy at No. 2 sure is. I think that was probably due to him being underpriced, but you can see only Julio Jones led to a worse win rate in cash games. I think it's really interesting to see only Jones with a sub-50-percent cash rate. This is more evidence that the crowd is generally getting it right in cash games; individual bias is factored out of overall usage rates, so we see a very high overall cash rate here, including as high as 65 percent with Jeremy Hill.

Let's compare cash games to GPPs...

Most Popular Players in DraftKings GPPs

Name	Position	% Used	Cash %
Jordy Nelson	WR	14.76%	28%
LeSean McCoy	RB	13.32%	19%
Le'Veon Bell	RB	12.51%	25%
Kelvin Benjamin	WR	12.06%	24%
Antonio Brown	WR	11.61%	27%
Steve Smith	WR	10.98%	22%
Odell Beckham	WR	10.89%	39%
Julius Thomas	TE	10.44%	22%
Julio Jones	WR	9.99%	19%
Jeremy Hill	WR	9.45%	32%

More wide receivers, which isn't a shocker. We still see a lot of the same names, with Julius Thomas actually replacing Rob Gronkowski as the top tight end.

And again, we see some really high cash rates (remember the average GPP cash rate is around 20 percent), including a ridiculous 39 percent from Beckham. Holy shit dude.

Now let's compare who was most popular to who was most profitable...

Highest Cash Rates in Cash Games

Name	Position	Cash %
Odell Beckham	WR	73%
Jeremy Hill	RB	65%
CJ Anderson	RB	64%
Lamar Miller	RB	63%
Aaron Rodgers	QB	62%
Jordy Nelson	WR	61%
Marshawn Lynch	RB	61%
Mark Sanchez	QB	60%
Marquess Wilson	WR	60%
AJ Green	WR	60%

I think we should collectively just agree to forget everything Beckham did in his rookie year. The difference between the percentage of cash games he won and that of the No. 2 player—Jeremy Hill—was still much larger than that between Hill and the next nine players. I think I played Beckham in cash games one time all year. Coincidentally, I lost a bit of money in December. It wasn't a great Christmas for the Bales family is all I'm saying. Beckham was so good that he turned Eli Manning into a top quarterback when he was in the lineup…

Highest Cash Rates in GPPs

Name	Position	Cash %
Odell Beckham	WR	39%
Eli Manning	QB	36%
Derek Anderson	QB	34%
Jeremy Hill	RB	32%
Harry Douglas	WR	32%
Marquess Wilson	WR	29%
CJ Anderson	RB	29%
Aaron Rodgers	QB	29%
Cardinals	DST	29%
Jordy Nelson	WR	28%

If you stacked ODB and Manning near the end of the season, you're probably not reading this because you're lying on the beach on your private island.

Flexing

When I first began playing DFS, I sucked. I didn't know what I was doing. I thought I would run all over the competition just from knowing football and I got crushed. I really had to take a step back from the I-know-what-I'm-doing mentality and embrace the fact that I had a whole lot to learn.

So I started learning the game—reading everything about daily fantasy I could get my hands on—and I decided I needed to find an edge somewhere, then build around that edge. Where was the DFS market going wrong, and how could I exploit that?

The area on which I settled was the flex position. I had plenty of experience exploiting the flex position in season-long leagues, and in both traditional and daily fantasy, the flex position is still mismanaged.

The flex is so important because it forces players to compare players not just within a position, but among them. Everyone has a decent idea of how Jeremy Hill's value compares to that of DeMarco Murray in a given week, but it's less obvious how Hill's value compares to that of, say, Randall Cobb. It's that lack of an obvious comparison that I think leads to an inefficiency.

I have a ton of thoughts on which positions are best for use in the flex in specific situations, but first let's get to the data. Here's a look at last year's flex usage and win rates in DraftKings cash games.

	Flex Data for Cash Games		
Position	Overall Usage	Usage By Cashing Lineups	Overall Cash %
RB	60.5%	64.2%	53.7%
WR	32.2%	30.6%	48.2%
TE	7.3%	5.2%	36.0%

Running back was the most popular flex position in cash games, used in 60.5 percent of all head-to-head and 50/50 lineups. Wide receivers were in a little more than half that amount, while tight ends were used in the flex in fewer than 1 in 13 lineups.

Only running backs were used in more cashing lineups than overall. If you used a running back as your flex in a cash game, you had roughly a 53.7 percent chance of cashing last year. Meanwhile, wide receivers led to a 48.2 percent cash rate—obviously slightly below what we'd expect randomly—and tight ends were absolutely horrible at just 36.0 percent.

There are two important items I want to mention. First, I think there could be at least somewhat of a selection bias here, with lineups that utilized a running back in the flex in cash games at least somewhat skewed toward better lineups overall.

The reason? My second point: running backs make sense in cash games because they have more predictable outcomes than receivers or tight ends. Their production is simply less volatile week to week due to heavier workloads, and thus more chances for their fantasy production to regress toward the mean.

And remember, narrowing the range of outcomes for your lineup is smart in cash games. It doesn't matter if you average 150 points per week if you score 200 points half the time and 100 points the other half; the distribution and deviation in your scores matters. Running backs squeeze down the distribution such that you create a higher floor for your lineup that ultimately aids in cash games, especially 50/50s.

That 53.7 percent cash rate is pretty high, too, when you consider there were certainly some poor running back selections in that sample. If you focus on specific types of running backs—namely those on teams favored to win and/or those who can catch a lot of passes—I think you can cut into your weekly volatility even more. Just from blindly selecting an appropriate running back for the flex, you might be looking at, say, a 55 percent expected winning percentage right out of the gate—not a bad starting point.

If you are thinking of starting a tight end in the flex in a cash game, do me a favor and challenge me in a head-to-head. Seriously though, there might be a time when it's okay to use a tight end in the flex, but he better be a once-in-a-season sort of value to make up for the volatility you need to take on.

As you'd expect, things are a bit different in GPPs…

		Flex Data for GPPs	
Position	Overall Usage	Usage By Cashing Lineups	Overall Cash %
RB	44.4%	45.6%	21.6%
WR	44.4%	44.9%	21.3%
TE	11.2%	9.4%	17.6%

Running backs and wide receivers were equally popular as tournament flex plays last season. Both positions were in more cashing lineups than overall, but barely.

Meanwhile, tight ends as a whole were again poor flex plays. However, tight end is such a unique position, with a couple elite guys and then everyone else. I think there's a case to be made for a Rob Gronkowski/Jimmy Graham pairing at times—especially to help differentiate a lineup—but otherwise, tight ends were not quality flex plays in any format last season.

I think it's important to note this is all price-dependent. Last year, we saw a small change in pricing that made running backs more attractive flex plays. Their prices dropped a tad to basically put them on an even playing field with receivers in terms of value (making them comparable GPP plays and better cash plays due to their predictable scoring patterns). If DraftKings changes their scoring, making one position cheaper as a whole, we'll need to adjust based on the shift in value.

"If you go back a few hundred years, what we take for granted today would seem like magic - being able to talk to people over long distances, to transmit images, flying, accessing vast amounts of data like an oracle. These are all things that would have been considered magic a few hundred years ago."

    Elon Musk

V. The Ultimate List of Daily Fantasy Football Heuristics

"This is the essence of intuitive heuristics: when faced with a difficult question, we often answer an easier one instead, usually without noticing the substitution."

Daniel Kahneman

Kurt Vonnegut said, "If you want to break the rules of grammar, first learn the rules of grammar." I think that's a wonderful analogy for decision-making in daily fantasy sports. Yes, there are times you should break the rules, siding against the long-term data because there are other more powerful reasons to choose or not choose a player. But if you're continually breaking the rules—if you consistently go against what is working over the long run—you're not going to win.

We see this all the time in the NFL, with many teams still forgoing the use of analytics in favor of the eye test. They basically hire a group of people to find exceptions to the rules, when they could probably beat their current success rates with one nerd running some numbers for them for a day. Everyone thinks *this* slow running back is the one to whom the numbers don't apply or that *this* small wide receiver will actually be able to score at a high rate in the red zone. And sometimes they do; but when you disregard heuristics completely, you get five Tavon Austins for every Marvin Harrison.

I like heuristics because I think they're a starting point for us as daily fantasy players. I'm not going to say I'll never stack a quarterback, running back, and receiver from the same team, but knowing that the combination has been a losing one overall—including just a 43.0 percent win rate in cash games—is important and should help guide my decision regarding whether or not *this* QB/RB/WR combo is the right one.

A heuristic is defined as "a technique for problem-solving and learning that finds a solution that, while not guaranteed to be optimal, speeds up the process of finding a satisfactory solution via mental shortcuts." We don't need certainty for a heuristic to be useful; they aren't true in every situation, but good enough to improve overall decision-making. I think this is a really important point that a lot of the every-situation-is-unique and stats-don't-tell-the-whole-story crowds miss; there are exceptions to every rule, but again, you're not going to have a lot of success if you're continually siding with those exceptions.

I think heuristics are useful in daily fantasy football because of the lack of predictability in the game. If we could more accurately predict which players will have monster games, for example, then it would make sense to more consistently break the general rule of "Pay up for top quarterbacks in cash games," for example. The week-to-week volatility in football makes the long-term trends—and the heuristics that are based off of them—more valuable.

Every rule is made to be broken, but if you don't know the rules, you can't successfully play the game.

DFS Strategy

1. Narrow your range of outcomes in cash games.

2. Widen your range of outcomes in GPPs.

3. All else equal, emphasize players with lower ownership in tournaments.

4. Be more contrarian at higher stakes and more price-sensitive at lower stakes.

5. For pure ROI, emphasize head-to-head games over high-stakes 50/50s.

6. Structure your bankroll as a reflection of your league selection.

7. Use the Bargain Rating at Fantasy Labs to identify underpriced players and shop for the best prices.

8. Target players whose salary has recently dropped (without an obvious reason it should have).

9. Don't target cold players who haven't seen a major change in price.

10. Emphasize projected workload before any other stats to find the most value.

11. Play the chalk to maximize the chances of cashing in tournaments, but be at least slightly contrarian to maximize the chances of winning.

12. If you have an under-the-radar player as a top value, use him as a foundational piece of your GPP lineups.

Position-Specific

13. Avoid quarterbacks in very cold and very windy games.

14. Target pass-catching running backs and wide receivers who see a lot of short targets if you want consistency.

15. Look for quarterbacks on underdogs still expected by Vegas to score a lot of points.

16. Target quarterbacks in non-division games and avoid those in division games late in the season.

17. Pay up for quarterbacks and running backs (especially the latter) in cash games and save money at the other positions.

18. Strongly consider paying for elite wide receivers in GPPs.

19. Use a running back in the flex in most cash-game lineups. A high-volume wide receiver is fine in many instances, but almost always avoid a tight end.

20. Consider both running backs and wide receivers for flex use in tournaments.

Stacking

21. Emphasize correlations in GPPs.

22. Avoid starting any player and the opposing defense.

23. Avoid starting two running backs on opposing teams.

24. Avoid QB/RB/WR in almost all situations.

25. Use QB/RB on explosive offenses, but only in cash games (upside limited in GPPs).

26. QB/WR is the most popular stack and very viable in GPPs, but avoid it in cash for the most part.

27. Avoid QB/WR/WR in cash games, but consider it on certain offenses for GPPs.

28. Avoid QB + 3 Receivers, which doesn't provide enough upside to mitigate the risk.

29. Consider RB + D as a smart pairing when the team is a favorite.

30. Consider not stacking at all for risk-minimization in cash games and to be contrarian in tournaments.

"I discourage passive skepticism, which is the armchair variety where people sit back and criticize without ever subjecting their theories or themselves to real field testing."

   Tim Ferriss

VI. Sample from "Daily Fantasy Pros Reveal Their Money-Making Secrets"

"Chance is commonly viewed as a self-correcting process in which a deviation in one direction induces a deviation in the opposite direction to restore the equilibrium. In fact, deviations are not "corrected" as a chance process unfolds, they are merely diluted."

Amos Tversky

Last year, I teamed up with a bunch of DFS pros to write a book called "Daily Fantasy Pros Reveal Their Money-Making Secrets."

Check out the chapter on advanced tournament play from Al_Smizzle.

Advanced Tournament Play with Al_Smizzle

Chicks dig the long ball, and in daily fantasy sports, GPPs are just that. Al_Smizzle knows what it's like to win $350,000 in a single daily fantasy football tournament, as he finished second in the 2013 DraftKings Millionaire Grand Final. He's widely considered one of the best tournament players in the world.

I spoke with "Smizz" about general tournament strategies and his approach to taking down daily fantasy football GPPs on DraftKings.

With the variance in tournaments, what percentage of your action (and your total bankroll) goes to GPPs?

It really depends on the day/week and the type of tournaments, but the most of my bankroll I'll ever really play at once is 10 percent. That's not just tournaments; that's money in play in all league types at one given time.

Then, I'll typically put about 80 to 90 percent of that into cash games—head-to-head, 50/50s, and so on. I actually prefer 50/50s the most just because there's some upside there too. But if you do the math, that's no more than 20 percent of my money that's in play in tournaments, GPPs, qualifiers, large-field leagues—whatever you want to call them—and just 10 percent of my money in play at once, max, which equates to no more than two percent of my entire bankroll being used for tournaments at any given time.

Some people are going to argue that I could be more aggressive, but I don't really think so, nor do I want to be. First of all, you can go on some pretty long cold streaks playing tournaments, and second, I chase a lot of qualifiers, which have the lowest short-term expected return since they're typically top-heavy and often award tickets instead of cash.

And again, that's a max—10 percent of the total bankroll in all games, two percent of the total bankroll in tournaments on any given day.

What's your process for creating your tournament lineups?

Well, I start with my cash game lineup. I usually play just one cash lineup per site. So on DraftKings, I'll make one lineup for head-to-head and 50/50 games that I like, and then I tend to build my tournament lineups around the core guys that I like from that lineup.

You want different traits in tournaments, for sure, but you still want exposure to the best values, which you're playing in your cash games. And few guys who have a high floor that you might play in a head-to-head also have a really low ceiling so that you wouldn't want to use them in a GPP.

I use that foundation in most tournament lineups, then I fill in based on the type of tournament. In a qualifier, you basically want to win the entire thing, depending how it's structured, so I want as much upside as possible. In that format, I'm looking for high-ceiling players, and I'll also be more likely to use a contrarian strategy. I'm really looking to finish first, even if it means that a large percentage of the time I'll have a really poor lineup.

In typical cash GPPs, the first thing I'm looking to do is cash. I want to use the core values that I've found to cash, then just hope that those guys can hit enough to also propel me up toward the top. But it's more about value and a combination of safety/upside for normal GPPs, whereas in qualifiers I want all upside.

Also, I map out a certain budget at the beginning of the year that I have set aside just for qualifiers. So a lot of my qualifier strategy—at least the number I enter—is dictated by that budget.

You mentioned being contrarian. Talk about that strategy and how much you use it.

Being contrarian means purposely going against the grain so that you can have a unique lineup, which can help win a tournament. Like I said, my main goal in most GPPs—the first thing I need to do—is just to cash. In that regard, I'm more of a value-based player than some other guys, so I just want pure value, regardless of ownership percentage. It doesn't matter to me if a player will be heavily utilized if he's the best value in a GPP. In qualifiers, I'm more contrarian-prone.

I don't mind going contrarian, but only if there's value there. I played Marvin Jones all over the place during his four-touchdown week in 2013, and he was like two percent owned (and I probably accounted for about half of that two percent in some tournaments). I didn't just play him because I thought others wouldn't, though; he had been getting more and more snaps and targets in the prior week, and I wanted to go high-priced at running back that week, so he just worked.

My strategy also changes a lot throughout the season. In the beginning of the year, I'm much more likely to be contrarian because everyone is basically picking players based off of season-long ADP, which is mostly based off of the prior season's stats. Football is such a unique sport in that some data from the previous year isn't really that meaningful, though; situations change, coaches change, personnel changes, so there aren't necessarily great numbers to use to determine team or player strength.

For that reason, I'm not as value-based early in the year just because it's more difficult to determine value. Then, I think there's a lot more value in going against the grain. As the season progresses, we get more and more data and we can see how certain players perform together or how coaches are calling things. By the end of the year, I care less about projected ownership because I think I can create more accurate values.

Do you normally go against the grain on low-priced options like Jones?

No, not necessarily. One thing I really like to do is pay up for high-priced studs who maybe don't have an ideal matchup. When you have a player like Calvin Johnson, it really doesn't matter who he's facing; he can go for 200 yards against anyone. But if he has a bad matchup, you'll see his usage plummet.

Sometimes you'll have studs who are in only five percent of lineups because of the matchup, and that's a great situation. You get an elite player and you get to be contrarian at the same time. With those guys, the price and value don't matter as much because they have so much upside no matter what.

In my head-to-head games, I'm searching for the players who have the most access to a realistic outcome—an attainable threshold of production. In tournaments, I want players who have the most access to elite outcomes, and players like Johnson, Jamaal Charles, and so on can have those games against any opponent.

How much does overlay matter to you?

It matters. I look at it, but I'm not going to go crazy chasing it. Some guys go way over their budget when they see overlay and it can end up killing them. It's not like you're just automatically going to cash when there's overlay. Even if a league fills up to only 80 percent, you're still going to see just 1-in-4 entrants cash, at the most, in the majority of tournaments.

I'll throw a couple extra lineups into a league when I see overlay because it's still a good situation, but you can't go over your budget. It more just changes how I structure my league selection; I'd be more inclined to place a higher percentage of my money into that league as opposed to putting extra money in on top of what I usually play.

Also, I consider overlay anything under the breakeven point for the site. Some people think that there's overlay if a 3,000-man tournament fills to only 2,900 entrants, but the site is still making money at that point, so you're −EV as an average player. Overlay is actually anything where the site is losing money on the league.

How do you structure your lineups with multi-entry? How much do you diversify?

It depends on the week, but I definitely diversify more than football than the other sports, particularly basketball. Football is really an event-based sport; the majority of the points come from basically one event—a touchdown—which can be really volatile from week to week. It's just difficult to predict who is going to score and how much, so that opens up the player pool a little bit.

I usually pick my core stacks that I like—usually one quarterback and one wide receiver—and then I build around those. I'll start with some players I use in my cash games, but I'll expand the player pool a bit. But it's not like I'm just picking everyone; it's about picking those core stacks and then building different player combinations around those.

That helps to make sure I actually cash if the stack hits. If I play a particular quarterback/wide receiver combination just once and they go off but the rest of the lineup around them doesn't do much, then I can't realize the potential of the stack. If I diversify more around that stack, I'll make sure that I hit with at least one of the combinations so that the stack doesn't get wasted, so to speak.

Discuss your stacking strategy and how you mix and match players.

Well, I'm almost always looking to pair a quarterback with at least one of his pass-catchers in a tournament. There's just so much upside to that strategy that you almost can't not do it. Sometimes I'll use a quarterback and two of his wide receivers or a wide receiver and tight end, but it depends on the team. That's a good strategy on high-scoring offenses like the Broncos; last year, we went into games pretty much knowing the Broncos would score four touchdowns, so there lots of upside in using the quarterback and two of his receivers. That's not the case on other teams.

Another type of stack that I like—and it isn't really a stack as much of just an optimal pairing—is using a running back and his defense. A lot of people overlook that, but a running back's play is correlated with the defense; if the defense does well, it probably means the team is winning, which will result in more late carries for the running back. That's a smart pairing that isn't that popular.

Another pairing that I like is a defense and kicker, particularly in games projected to be close and low-scoring. Lots of times, we'll see defensive battles where a team's defense is winning the field position battle and providing great opportunities to the offense, but they can't punch it in and need to settle for field goals. In those situations, you'll see a high correlation between defensive points and field goals. A lot of players want to start kickers on great offenses, but if they score a bunch of touchdowns, those field goal opportunities can disappear.

How about QB-RB-WR? Is there ever a good time to use that trio?

I wouldn't say that I never use a quarterback with his wide receiver and running back, but it's not common. It really depends on the situation; I might do it with Matt Forte or someone like that who can catch a lot of passes so that his play is correlated to the quarterback. But if a running back can't catch passes and score on those receptions, it's tough to get him in there in a stack.

It's kind of like using a hitter against the opposing pitcher in baseball. It's not impossible that the pitcher and hitter both have a great game, but it's not likely because their production is inversely correlated. In most cases, you just wouldn't be playing the percentages. It's not that it *can't* work, just that it isn't optimal.

How does the PPR format on a site like DraftKings affect your GPP approach?

Oh man, it really changes how I build a lineup. Even the difference between full PPR and 0.5 PPR is huge. I think it's obvious that there are players who are naturally better-suited for point-per-reception leagues than others—guys like Antonio Brown—but it also should change the way you construct your lineup in general.

On DraftKings, for example, you need to start someone in the flex spot. Wide receivers have a lot more merit as flex options in PPR leagues than standard scoring. I think those guys who catch a lot of passes and, specifically, see a lot of targets are the ones who are also the most predictable from week to week. So those targets are something that I really pay for on a PPR site.

Speaking of the flex, how do you handle it in tournaments? Do you always play a particular position?

No, I don't always play one position. Basically, the main thing I want to do with the flex is use the player who is playing in the latest game (among the players that I like). So I select my players—whether it's three running backs or three receivers (with one in the flex)—and then I just use the player who has the latest possible game in the flex.

To give you an idea why I do that, I'll tell you about the DraftKings Millionaire Grand Final. Heading into the Monday night game, there were basically two players who could win the $1 million grand prize—me and a player named bundafever. He was up by less than two points heading into the game and we each had one player left.

Bundafever's lone player was a running back. Looking at his guys who had already played and their salaries, I was able to reverse-engineer his lineup to figure out that he almost certainly had Frank Gore as his running back.

The problem was that I also had Gore, so the only way that I could catch him was to do a late swap to get Gore out of my lineup. Luckily, I placed Gore in the flex spot, so I was able to switch to Michael Crabtree. I still would have been able to do a late swap if I had Gore in my running back spot, but I would have needed to switch to a backup running back. Plus, by using Crabtree, I knew I'd have a unique lineup since bundafever had a running back, so I could potentially catch him. On the flip side, bundafever used Gore in the running back spot. If the standings were reversed and I had been ahead, he couldn't have swapped to Crabtree.

It didn't work out for me that time—I finished second and won $350,000—but the move gave me lots of different options.

The other thing that I like to do with the flex spot is use any player who might be listed as questionable. Obviously I'm not going to start someone if I think he'll be out, but sometimes guys are late scratches. If there's someone who I really like but he's questionable, I'll sometimes use him as the flex because, if he doesn't play, I'll have more options because I can sub to a bunch of different positions instead of just one.

Do you ever pay up for defenses?

I'll pay for defenses that I like. Defenses can go a long way in determining tournament success, and they aren't as unpredictable as everyone thinks. Also, most people go with near-min-priced defenses, so paying a little more can help you field a unique lineup; it's a way to be contrarian without really using a sub-optimal strategy from a value standpoint.

Which traits/stats do you look for when selecting tournament lineups?

The main thing I look at is defensive vs. position stats. Those aren't as valuable in the beginning of the year (or else you need to use last year's stats), but they're more valuable by midseason or so. A lot of players look at the overall quality of a defense, but there are some good defenses that really struggle against one particular position, or bad defenses that can defend one position well. The Cardinals have had a decent defense recently but just can't stop the tight end, for example.

As far as finding particular players, one stat that I really like is 'percentage of supply.' Basically, I want to know what percentage of his team's targets a wide receiver or tight end eats up, or what percentage of carries a running back gets. I think that's a lot more valuable than most bulk stats. When a player receives a heavy workload and he's facing off against a defense that struggles against his position, that's usually a situation I want to target.

CSURAM88's Analysis

The contrarian versus value topic is my favorite when it comes to tournaments. I think it's a really delicate issue that you need to balance because, all other things equal, you want the best values in your lineup. "All other things" aren't always equal, though, so going against the grain is smart at times.

I think it's still really more of an art than a science at this point. Part of that is because you don't really know for sure what usage rates will look like prior to entering a tournament. You might have a decent idea of which players will be the most heavily utilized, but there are always surprises. Without knowing utilization exactly, you're left guessing, so that adds a little incentive to just go with the top values if you're unsure.

When it's very clear that a particular player or stack is going to be really heavily utilized, then I think it comes down to other factors, like the number of lineups you're submitting. If you have a bunch of entries into a tournament, you of course want some exposure to the "chalk," whereas players with just a single entry or two really need to consider a contrarian strategy a lot more seriously. If you have just a single shot to take down a tournament, you really want that lineup to be a unique one.

"Basically if you study entrepreneurs, there is a misnomer: People think that entrepreneurs take risk, and they get rewarded because they take risk. In reality entrepreneurs do everything they can to minimize risk. They are not interested in taking risk. They want free lunches and they go after free lunches."

Mohnish Pabrai

Postface

The End.

Some Special Offers and Free Stuff

For readers of this book, I have five special offers...

100% Bonus on DraftKings + Free Game

If you sign up and deposit on DraftKings, you'll immediately get a 100% deposit bonus up to $600. That's up to $600 for free just for signing up and depositing.

And use the promo code 'Bales' for free entry into a paid game.

Free Trial + 50% Off at Fantasy Labs

Fantasy Labs is my baby. If you don't already use it, you're absolutely going to love it. I teamed up with one of the best daily fantasy sports players in the world in CSURAM88, and we have an amazing development team. We've created a bunch of tools to help you win at DFS, the coolest of which is called Player Models—a simple-to-use tool that allows you to weigh all sorts of stats to create (and backtest) your own models, then optimize lineups off of your models. Even novice players can immediately create league-winning models, rankings, and lineups because we show you what actually works.

It's incredible, and I'm giving away a free trial and 50% off the first month. Just go to FantasyLabs.com and enter the code 'BALESBOOK' on the payment page to start your free trial.

A Free DFS Guide

I have a short e-book called *A Guide to Winning at Daily Fantasy Sports*. It contains some excerpts from other books and a bunch of new content as well. You can download it for free at http://eepurl.com/buuZWj.

10% Off Everything On My Site

If you want to purchase any of the other books in my Fantasy Sports for Smart People book series (or one of the other products I offer), you can do that at FantasyFootballDrafting.com. If you head over there, use the coupon code "Smart10" at checkout to get 10% off your entire order.

Free Course from RotoAcademy—My Daily Fantasy Training Marketplace

Finally, I'm giving away a free premium course from RotoAcademy. I teamed up with RotoGrinders to build RotoAcademy, which is a marketplace for premium DFS education. We sell entire courses, each made up of between four and 12 lessons designed to help you master a specific area of daily fantasy strategy. It's a fantastic way to supplement the data and advice you'll get from this book.

Head over to RotoGrinders.com/RotoAcademy to check it out. If you see a course you like, again, just email me at fantasyfootballdrafting@gmail.com (or tweet me @BalesFootball) and I'll send it to you for free.

Before taking off, I want to say thanks to DraftKings for all the help in putting this book together, as well as Ian Hartitz, who has helped me collect data over the years, and of course my good friend Jaden Smith.

24348589R00106

Made in the USA
Middletown, DE
21 September 2015